Stakeholding and New Labour

Stakeholding and New Labour

Rajiv Prabhakar
Ludwig Lachmann Fellow
Department of Philosophy, Logic and Scientific Method
London School of Economics

palgrave
macmillan

First published 2003 by
PALGRAVE MACMILLAN
Houndmills, Basingstoke, Hampshire RG21 6XS and
175 Fifth Avenue, New York, N.Y. 10010
Companies and representatives throughout the world

PALGRAVE MACMILLAN is the global academic imprint of the Palgrave Macmillan division of St. Martin's Press, LLC and of Palgrave Macmillan Ltd. Macmillan® is a registered trademark in the United States, United Kingdom and other countries. Palgrave is a registered trademark in the European Union and other countries.

ISBN 1–4039–0360–3

This book is printed on paper suitable for recycling and made from fully managed and sustained forest sources.

A catalogue record for this book is available from the British Library.

Library of Congress Cataloging-in-Publication Data
Prabhakar, Rajiv, 1970–
Stakeholding and New Labour / Rajiv Prabhakar.
p. cm.
Includes bibliographical references and index.
ISBN 1–4039–0360–3
1. Great Britain – Economic conditions – 1997– 2. Great Britain – Economic policy – 1997– 3. Industrial relations – Great Britain. 4. Great Britain – Politics and government – 1997– 5. Keynesian economics. I. Title.

HC256.7.P7 2003
330.941–dc21 2002193084

10 9 8 7 6 5 4 3 2 1
12 11 10 09 08 07 06 05 04 03

Printed and bound in Great Britain by
Antony Rowe Ltd, Chippenham and Eastbourne

To my mother and father

Contents

Preface

In 1996 Will Hutton published *The State We're In*. This advocated 'stakeholder capitalism' as a way of reforming the British economy. This book provoked much interest and had a large impact on political discussions. Hutton's criticisms of Conservative party policy since 1979 captured the public mood, and his book topped best-seller lists. His claim to provide an alternative to the strategies previously adopted by Conservative and Labour parties caught the imagination of academics interested in charting a 'third way'. In 1996 Tony Blair, the leader of the Labour party, made a high-profile speech in Singapore claiming that stakeholding was to be New Labour's 'big idea'. Stakeholding, however, provoked fierce criticism. Some claimed it was incoherent. Others said it offered nothing new – on the right it was seen as displaying the worst parts of 'old Labour', on the left as a capitulation to Thatcherism. New Labour's references to stakeholding were scaled down. Many concluded that stakeholding fell from New Labour's radar screen almost as swiftly as it had first appeared.

This book challenges much of this received wisdom and is conducted on two main fronts. It argues, first, that stakeholding is a more subtle and complex set of ideas than many of its critics supposed. Although Hutton helped popularise stakeholding, other models were also developed. Stakeholding is in fact robust to the arguments of many of its critics, while also offering a genuine alternative to policies previously deployed by Labour and the Conservatives. Second, although explicit references to stakeholding have been scaled down, stakeholding remains important for understanding the ideas and the policies of New Labour in government. Important parts of New Labour's first-term agenda overlap with stakeholder ideas. These are being consolidated and expanded in its second term. The book analyses the ideas of the main contributors to stakeholder debates (both supporters and critics). Since stakeholding attracted individuals from a variety of backgrounds, such as politicians, journalists and academics (who themselves came from different disciplines), as well as policy commissions, the book looks at all these different actors. A distinctive feature is that the book brings together for the first time the debates on stakeholding in different areas, such as corporate governance and public services. The exploration of New Labour looks at both theory and policy. In relation to theory, the pamphlets, speeches and writings of individuals such as Tony Blair, Anthony Giddens, and Peter Mandelson are explored. For policy, the book looks at green and white papers, treasury spending plans and commitments, and general election manifesto pledges.

Acknowledgements

I have acquired a variety of debts during the writing of this book. The Department of Politics and the Political Economy Research Centre at the University of Sheffield proved to be a very supportive environment in which to work. I would like to thank all those connected with these institutions. Sylvia McColm and Sarah Cooke both deserve particular mention for the secretarial and administrative support they have furnished. I would also like to thank my new colleagues at the Department of Philosophy, Logic and Scientific Method at the London School of Economics for their support for my research.

I am very grateful for financial support from the Economic and Social Research Council. This is on two counts. The first relates to a doctoral studentship that funded the research upon which the book is based. Secondly, I am pleased to acknowledge assistance under the ESRC's post-doctoral fellowship scheme. This provided support in turning my research into a book. I am also grateful for financial assistance from the Charlottenburg Trust (which funds my Lachmann fellowship) during the latter stages of the production of this book.

My greatest intellectual debt is to Andrew Gamble. He supervised the research upon which this volume is based. His searching questions and critical comments often put me right and helped clarify my thinking. On a different level, his encouragement and good humour made the passage of my research very much easier. His contribution has been invaluable. Debts are also owed to Sue Bowden, Ralf Dahrendorf, Mathew Festenstein, Frank Field, Stephen George, Mike Kenny, Steve Ludlam, David Marquand, Jonathan Perraton, and John Plender. All of these, in different capacities, helped inform my thinking about the issues raised here. Martin Smith deserves special thanks for his role as my ESRC post-doctoral fellowship scheme mentor. He oversaw the writing of this book, being generous with both his time and effort. His advice has been very helpful in the completion of the work. I am also grateful to Alison Howson at Palgrave Macmillan for her support, as well as comments received from two readers there. These helped improve the book's form and content. One of these referees, Stuart White, who eventually waived his anonymity, deserves special thanks for his very helpful comments and suggestions. I have tried, as far as possible, to do justice to the comments received from all of the above. I would also like to thank Anne Rafique for her swift and efficient copy-editing. Any remaining errors are, of course, my own.

I would like to thank the editors of the following journals for permission to draw (often in heavily revised form) on some of the material I have previously had published: 'Education, markets and tacit knowledge', *Economic Affairs*, 22(2) (2002); 'The Idea of a Stake', *Politics*, 19(3) (1999); 'Social capital, stakeholder capitalism and the third way', *Renewal*, 7(3) (1999); and 'Governance and Stakeholding: how different are the shareholder and stakeholder models?', *New Economy*, 5(2) (1998).

On a personal level, I would particularly like to thank my mother, father, brother and Helen Ward. I would also like to thank Rusal Bostan, Cormac Hollingsworth, Frank McMahon and David Richardson. All of these made the process of writing this book much easier.

1
The State We're In

During the 1990s stakeholder arguments provoked a lot of interest across a variety of fields. Popular interest was indicated by the success of works such as Will Hutton's *The State We're In* (Hutton 1996).[1] Unusually for a work of public policy, this book topped best-seller lists, reflecting a mood for change as well as helping to secure the place of stakeholding within public debates within this period. Alongside his journalism at *The Guardian* and *The Observer* newspapers (Goldblatt 1999), *The State We're In* operated as a reflection on the state of the nation after fifteen years of unbroken Conservative rule at a national level. Hutton suggested that rather than addressing problems, Conservatives had actually perpetuated, and in some cases exacerbated, failures of British capitalism. At a political level stakeholder ideas were taken up by Tony Blair, the leader of Britain's main opposition to the Conservative party. This was signalled in, for example, a high-profile speech that Blair made to the Singapore business community on 8 January 1996. Stakeholding seemed central to Blair's attempts to recast Labour as 'New Labour'. This occurred at a time when Labour seemed destined for government, creating the possibility that stakeholding would help define Labour's programme in office. Stakeholding also provoked interest within the academy, drawing together academics from different backgrounds. Individuals from different disciplines such as politics, economics, business studies and social policy all expressed interest in stakeholder ideas. Some suggested the creation of a new intellectual framework.

David Marquand argued,

> the late 1980s and early 1990s saw a remarkable ferment of ideas on the British left and centre left. Writers such as Will Hutton, John Gray, John Kay, Ralf Dahrendorf and Harold Perkin began to grope towards a new intellectual and political paradigm, combining insights from traditional social liberalism and traditional social democracy. There were differences between them, but the notions of a stakeholder economy, a public domain and a pluralistic polity were common to nearly all. The Social Justice Commission, set up by John Smith, and the Dahrendorf Commission, set up by Paddy Ashdown, struck essentially the same chords. (Marquand 2000, p. 29)

Stakeholding attracted attention because it seemed potentially to constitute a new policy framework. It pointed to a set of organising principles that could fashion and help unite different interventions in public policy.

Background

Keynesian social democracy

Considering the background to stakeholding helps understand its nature and potential importance. From 1945 to the mid-1970s, 'Keynesian social democracy' defined the main parameters of centre-left politics in Britain. Although not endorsed by all reformers, most centre-left discussions bore its imprint. This combined a focus on social democracy with Keynesian economics. Anthony Crosland provided an important rationale for this combination (Crosland 1956). For Crosland social democracy was principally about ends (in particular, equality of opportunity). He thought that changes in the nature of capitalism implied that the means adopted to secure social democratic ends had to be rethought. In contrast to the historical emphasis on public ownership, the separation of ownership and control in modern corporations meant that issues of ownership were increasingly irrelevant. The nature of capital–labour relationships had also been transformed. Historically, capital was perceived to be dominant over both labour and government. This dominance no longer existed and so the nature of social democracy had to alter.

Trade unions that represented labour had emerged as important counterweights to capital. The growth in the size of the state, furthermore, furnished an agency capable of intervening and altering the shape of capital–labour relations. Using data on public expenditure as a percentage of gross national product as a measure of government intervention, Alan Peacock and Jack Wiseman suggest a significant growth in public expenditure in the United Kingdom during the twentieth century. From 12.7 per cent in 1910 this rose during the the First World War, reaching 35 per cent in 1915. Although this fell back to 24.4 per cent in 1935, it rose again during the Second World War. From 66 per cent in 1945 it fell back to 39 per cent in 1950. In this era, therefore, public expenditure more than tripled (charts A6 and A17, Peacock and Wiseman 1961). Leaving aside military expenditure, the corresponding figures for these years were 9.2 per cent in 1910, 8.8 per cent in 1915, 21.3 per cent in 1935. Data for 1945 are not available, though the figure was 31.8 per cent in 1950. Spending had similarly tripled.

Though state intervention could be governed by a variety of principles, Crosland drew from Keynesian economics. Rather than seeing markets as self-correcting, John Maynard Keynes suggested they were susceptible to various types of coordination failure. Involuntary unemployment was an important example of this. This occurred when individuals were willing, but unable, to find employment. Lack of consumer demand meant firms would be reluctant to expand production. Employment would not be offered, accordingly, to the unemployed. But, without jobs, the unemployed would rein back consumption, which in turn reinforced company strategies of retrenchment. Keynes suggested that state spending could help rectify this. Government expenditure would increase demand, causing firms to expand production and employ unemployed workers. Then consumer demand would rise as newly employed individuals would increase consumer demand, further supporting a rise in production (Keynes 1936). State spending was directed thus at achieving full employment under Keynesian social democracy. More generally the government also funded and provided welfare services. On this basis, institutions such as the National Health Service were established, providing an underpinning for social rights. For Crosland, securing equality of opportunity implied focusing on background endowments to secure a level playing field, especially in education and health. While Keynesian social democracy did not rely exclusively on the state, the central thrust of its policy prescriptions nevertheless did involve a focus on the state.

Free market reaction

Keynesian social democracy helped shape the policies of Labour governments. Building on a period of rapid growth in the world economy after the Second World War, Keynesian social democracy helped deliver low unemployment and universal welfare provision with low inflation. Conservative governments, in spite of various significant reservations and criticisms, deployed important aspects of Keynesian social democracy in this period. This became known as an era of 'consensus' politics.[2] By the mid-1970s, Keynesian social democracy began, however, to run into substantial difficulties. On a policy level, rather than reducing unemployment, Keynesian demand management techniques seemed only to help stoke up inflation. This combination of high unemployment and inflation became known as stagflation. The role of the welfare state in resolving welfare problems was also increasingly called into question. It was suggested, for example, that welfare state provision fuelled a dependency culture that exacerbated, rather than resolved, welfare problems. Here it was thought that individual responsibility was eroded as individuals came to rely solely on the state to address their welfare needs. For example if individuals were made unemployed, they depended on the state to provide them with a generous level of benefit. But this blunted their incentive to go and find work. The result of this was that unemployment lasted longer than it would have done had people taken more responsibility for finding work rather than expecting the state to bail them out. By fostering dependency, state intervention perpetuated problems such as unemployment. Tackling the dependency culture meant inculcating or restoring a sense of personal responsibility. Individuals, for instance, would be held more responsible for searching for work if made unemployed (Mead 1986). Allied to the sense of policy failure were increasingly strident intellectual attacks. Originating from a variety of sources, free market criticisms acquired particular significance. Part of these criticisms was rooted in efficiency concerns. For Hayek, much of economic activity rests on individually based 'tacit knowledge'. Tacit knowledge refers to the knowledge individuals acquire through 'learning by doing', which cannot be easily written down. For Hayek this 'know-how' is central for achieving efficiency. However, a centralised state cannot get access to this knowledge (it is only available to individuals through their practical experience). State intervention, therefore, is bound to be inefficient (Hayek 1967). Public choice theorists applied the methods of orthodox economics to the political realm to construct a series of models that pointed to inefficiency within social democracy. Orthodox economics sees all forms of reality in terms of individuals. As Andrew Gamble argues, this means that all actions

> are performed by individuals; therefore analysis of social reality must start from individuals, conceived as self-sufficient, fixed entities confronting the external world and responding to its opportunities and constraints by making choices and devising strategies ... [and] A social collective has no existence and no reality beyond the actions of its individual members.
>
> (Gamble 1996a, p. 53)

This is tied to a particular set of behavioural assumptions. Jon Elster notes that this means, first, that individual choices are intended to maximise personal happiness. This occurs when choices satisfy personal preferences. Given that individuals usually have some uncertainty about the happiness associated with particular choices, they set out to maximise expected happiness. Second, an individual's preferences only take their private interests into account. Lastly, individuals are rational in the sense of choosing the best means available to help realise their preferences (Elster 1996). Public choice theorists applied these assumptions to suggest that there are important inefficiencies associated with democracy. This means that social democracy, with its attachment to democracy, also furnishes inefficiency. A central charge is that democracy leads to bloated government. Democracy is analysed in terms of the decisions and actions of three principal actors: politicians, voters and bureaucrats. Politicians stand for office. Voters elect them for office. Once in power, bureaucrats implement their policies. The different actors each have different objectives they wish to maximise. In order to be elected, politicians wish to maximise the number of votes they receive. Voters wish to maximise the net benefits they enjoy from government services. Net benefits are the total benefits that accrue to each voter less the tax burden they have to bear in order to pay for these services. Bureaucrats are driven to maximise their bureaucratic empire in order to 'feather their nests'. The conjunction of the rational self-interested pursuit of these objectives leads to overextended government. Politicians have an incentive to outbid each other in their promises to the electorate in order to attract votes. The cost–benefit calculations entered into by voters are biased towards over-demand of services. Decisions are efficient when benefits exceed costs. In order for voters to make efficient choices, they have to consider all the costs and benefits associated with their choices. The costs of demanding a service, however, are spread over the whole tax-paying population. This means that voters do not face all the costs associated with their demands. They will find it worthwhile to demand a level of service beyond that which they would ask for if they had to take all costs into account. This fuels the excessive demand for services. As a result, voters are prone to respond to inflated promises. Bureaucrats do not put a check on this tendency of politicians to promise, and voters to demand, greater levels of government intervention, since this promotes the building of bureaucratic empires. The result is that the democratic process leads to a tendency for government to expand beyond the efficient level of intervention (Tullock 1976). William Niskanen's model of bureaucratic over-expansion is an example of a public choice critique. Niskanen argues that self-interest rather than an ethic of public service primarily motivates bureaucrats. They try to increase both the budget and the size of the office in which they work. This is because such growth helps to safeguard job security and provides opportunities for career progression and patronage. Civil servants can help ensure bureaucratic expansion through the role they play in fashioning the policy options and priorities discussed by government ministers (Niskanen 1971).

These critics endorsed, instead, free markets based on private property and the competitive search for profits as the central organising principle of economic and social life (Hayes 1994). Markets for Hayek promoted efficiency since they minimised the informational requirements for economic activity. Free markets for public choice theorists were best placed to coordinate self-interested motivations to secure efficiency, private vices here led by an invisible hand to the public good. Part of the criticisms of Keynesian social democracy reflected moral concerns. For Hayek the emphasis on social justice within social democracy was a mirage. He argued that only intentional decisions could be subject to moral scrutiny. Market outcomes were the unintended consequences of private economic decisions made by actors within a market. Inequality that arose in markets, though perhaps unfortunate, was not a matter for justice since it did not reflect intentional action. Moreover, within a society with individuals with diverse preferences there was unlikely to be agreement over just outcomes, and the result would simply be moral conflict. Emphasis should be placed instead on processes, concentrating simply on markets (Hayek 1976). These free-market arguments acquired importance at a political level by becoming a central theme of Conservative party policy during the 1980s and early 1990s. Although lacking majority electoral support, splits between their mainstream rivals and the workings of the first-past-the-post electoral system meant the Conservative party monopolised government from 1979 to 1997. The Conservative party was so successful at winning general elections that the prospect of one-party government was raised in some quarters (Margetts and Smyth 1994). Conservative party policy, particularly under Margaret Thatcher, was aimed at undermining the assumptions and institutions of Keynesian social democracy. Although there is controversy over the extent to which the Thatcher governments represented a coherent philosophy rather than being driven by pragmatism, in addition to disputes over the extent to which Thatcher succeeded in overturning important elements of Keynesian social democracy, it is nevertheless the case that the advance of important parts of a Keynesian social democratic agenda were either halted or reversed. In its place, greater focus was placed on the use of free markets. Privatisation was an important example of such a shift. Although there is evidence to suggest that the origins of privatisation lay more in pragmatic than in ideological factors, it nonetheless represented a substantially different set of policy outcomes and directions (Kavanagh 1997). In addition to selling off state assets to the private sector, privatisation encompassed the introduction of markets in service areas through, for example, contracting out, performance-related pay and value-for-money reviews (Vickers and Yarrow 1988).

Left responses

Keynesian social democracy faced a comprehensive assault, therefore, on a policy, intellectual and electoral front. One reaction to this from the left was simply to repudiate these free market criticisms. Although there was shared discontent with Keynesian social democracy, this emerged from the view that the principles of a planned economy had not been sufficiently applied. More, rather than less, planned intervention was required. This built upon a set of ideas first articulated within the context of an alternative economic strategy during the 1970s (such as in Holland 1975). This view acquired political importance since it helped define Labour's manifesto at the 1983 general election. An isolationist national economic policy organised around import controls, nationalisation and domestic reflation was espoused (Shaw 1994). The build-up to such a stance played an important role in prompting several senior Labour politicians including Roy Jenkins, Shirley Williams, William Rodgers and David Owen to leave the party and form the alternative Social Democratic party (SDP). At the 1983 general election, Labour suffered its worst post-war electoral performance, only narrowly avoiding coming in third place behind the SDP–Liberal alliance (although the nature of the electoral system meant Labour's share of seats was much higher than that of the alliance) (Butler and Kavanagh 1984). There was a possibility that Labour might be eclipsed as the main opposition to the Conservatives. In addition to these electoral problems, the policy credibility of this response was undermined by external developments. The failure in France of President Mitterrand's programme of rupturing with capitalism that was organised along similar lines weakened the view that this left response was viable in modern conditions (Lordon 1998). This was later compounded by the collapse of state socialism in the former USSR and Eastern Europe in the late 1980s and early 1990s.

Free-market criticisms were taken more seriously by centre-left reformers. David Marquand noted, 'Hayek was right. Governments don't and can't know enough to re-make society in accordance with a grand design, since no conceivable grand design can do justice to the complexity and reflexivity of human behaviour' (Marquand 1998a, p.11). Anthony Giddens also highlighted the importance of Hayek's informational critique of social democracy (Giddens 1998). Growing acceptance was also placed on the idea that public intervention within social democracy had relied too heavily on an ethic of public service on the part of public officials and neglected the importance of self-interested motivations (Le Grand 1997). Raymond Plant argues that legitimate concerns were raised about equality. He argues that although Crosland emphasised the importance of equality, he provided few arguments in favour of it. Plant traces this mainly to Crosland's underlying philosophical commitments. He argues that Crosland subscribed to the view that 'we cannot give philosophical foundations for our value commitments' (Plant 1996, p.172). It is not possible to ground personal viewpoints at the level of philosophical principles. No standard exists, therefore, to adjudicate between a set of different views. This meant for Crosland that 'there could be no decisive arguments for a particular set of political values, including his own' (ibid.). For Plant this helped condition Crosland's strategy for equality. Crosland could not embark on a strategy of persuasion given that no decisive arguments could be furnished for his position. His commitment to equality could only be imposed on individuals. The problem with this was that when sentiments were expressed against this, no strong arguments existed to fend off these attacks. The penetration of equality within public policy was therefore insecure, not robust. For Plant the logic of Crosland's position meant that equality could easily be challenged.

Modernisation

The combined force of these arguments dealt a heavy blow to centre-left politics. For these reformers, if centre-left politics was to have any sort of future, it had to be thoroughly reconstructed. This task began in earnest around the mid-1980s. One dimension to this involved a growing challenge to free markets. At an intellectual level, against the free-market emphasis on individualism, the importance of a collective ethos and institutions was affirmed (Marquand 1988). Julian Le Grand argued that though the public choice view that social democracy had placed too little emphasis on the importance of self-interested motivations was important, the free-market view that attention should only be paid to self-interested motivations when constructing policy was flawed. Public intervention had, in some part, to rely on an ethic of public service. As such, traditional social democratic emphases were still relevant. Raymond Plant contested

Hayek's critique of social justice, arguing that although market outcomes are unintended, they can nevertheless be foreseen. This is important because as long as the consequences are foreseen, they can be a matter of justice (Plant 1996). Free market policies were also criticised. Free markets were associated, for example, with an increase in inequality. In addition to undermining social cohesion, inequality was thought to foster inefficiency: it was, for example, thought to prevent an important section of the population from making a productive contribution because they lacked the resources to help engage in productive activity (Glyn and Miliband 1994).

An effective challenge to free markets, however, could only be mounted by forming an alternative programme. But for many centre-left reformers, this was not represented by a return to Keynesian social democracy. If the centre-left was to survive, it had to modernise. The search began, thus, for a centre-left alternative to free markets and Keynesian social democracy. This raised questions about the nature of centre-left reformism, for most of the twentieth-century reformists, especially social democrats, have placed emphasis on economic or social reform over political reform. This originated in the view that the most important issues facing society were economic and social in character. This focused especially on the relationship between capital and labour. Political reform was largely seen as a distraction. David Marquand argues this was reflected in the most influential post-war account of social rights. T. H. Marshall saw an emphasis on social rights as the culmination of a struggle to provide citizenship rights. Whereas the eighteenth and nineteenth centuries had respectively secured civil (such as freedom of expression) and political (such as voting) rights, the twentieth century had given rise to an emphasis on the provision of social rights (ensuring, for example, that individuals had adequate health provision). The implication of this for Marshall was that matters of civil and political rights were largely settled, and that social and economic issues ought to be the prime focus for debate (Marquand 1997; Marshall 1950). Little attention was paid to the processes through which policy was conducted. On this view stress was placed simply on capturing the state, and using this to pursue an economic and social agenda. This pointed to the use of mechanical 'top-down' reform. Following Peter Clarke, this refers to the top-down imposition of policy. Clarke argues, the 'mechanical reformist takes a pessimistic view of human nature; he has little faith in the capacity of the people to effect the necessary reforms of the system; but he knows on a scientific basis what progress ought to be; and he thinks that it can be achieved by substituting a mechanical for a moral means, to achieve what the people are incapable of doing for themselves' (Clarke 1978, p. 65). There existed, however, an alternative tradition that gave greater weight to the political realm. This emanated from the view that process and policy were inextricably linked. Greater attention was placed on 'bottom-up' reform. In this book bottom-up reform is understood to cover those attempts to encourage the direct participation of individuals in locally based arenas. Rather than being passive subjects of policy, individuals are actively involved in the policy process. Within each town or city, for example, Citizens' Juries could be established to discuss initiatives across the whole range of local services (such as schools, hospitals and leisure facilities). These juries are bodies that contain representatives (possibly elected) of users of local services. Local authorities would have a duty to consult with and take proper account of these juries when setting policy priorities and making budgetary decisions. Policy steps might only be implemented, for instance, once they won the approval of the appropriate jury. Another example concerns recycling organisations. These are local bodies that are responsible for developing recycling strategies (covering paper, bottles and cans, for instance) in a particular area. They are staffed and run by local residents (with financial support from the local council) and would be responsible for setting up and maintaining collection points (perhaps also arranging for collection for elderly or infirm residents). While the above are instances of individual activity within the context of collective organisations, bottom-up reform also encompasses participation on a more narrowly individualistic basis. Government, for example, could provide individuals with money which people would then use for various investments within the marketplace (such as helping pay for a deposit on a house or for an evening class). The focus overall is on individual participation in a variety of market and grassroots realms.

Bottom-up reform rests on an optimistic view of individuals. Peter Clarke argues that on an 'optimistic view progress can be assumed. A moral change, a change of heart, a new consciousness, will be the agent and sanction of a transformation within society'

(Clarke 1978, p. 5). Although reformist strategies contained elements of both, reformist strategies were nevertheless typically skewed in favour of either top-down or bottom-up reform. Top-down reformers encompassed individuals such as Sydney and Beatrice Webb and Anthony Crosland; bottom-up reformers included individuals such as R. H. Tawney (Marquand 1999a). Top-down reformism was the dominant reformist strategy throughout the twentieth century, as a result of the general priority placed on economic and social issues and the inability of bottom-up reformers to muster sufficient support. Keynesian social democracy was seen as an important example of top-down reform. An important part of the failure of Keynesian social democracy by those centre-left reformers who contributed to stakeholding was ascribed to its lack of focus on bottom-up reform. David Marquand, for example, suggested that part of the controversy surrounding social rights resulted from a complacent social democratic belief that previous debates over civil and political rights were adequately settled (Marquand 1997). In contrast he argued that the nature of political rights was not adequately settled. Social rights had to result from deliberation in the political realm, else they would rest on insecure foundations and be susceptible to easy challenge. This, he argued, was demonstrated by free-market criticisms. Responding to this required greater attention to be paid to the political realm, and to bottom-up reform.

Catch-up

Some claimed, however, that such reformism constituted a capitulation to free markets, whatever the rhetoric to the contrary. This meant, most obviously, an increasing acceptance of free-market proposals. Critics drew particular attention to the growing role the market played in these reformist accounts. Colin Hay offers the strongest version of this critique in his claim that this brand of reformism amounts to a politics of 'catch-up', where centre-left reformers catch up to the free-market settlement articulated by Conservatives (Hay 1999). Hay argues centre-left reformers should, in contrast, buck this trend. He supports a restatement of top-down reform, built in particular around the state. Colin Hay and Matthew Watson regard underinvestment in manufacturing capital as the key failing of British capitalism. Though not advocating a return to Keynesian social democracy, they endorse the foundation of a new state tradition that would foster investment in the domestic manufacturing industry (Hay and Watson 1998).

But use of markets does not necessarily imply that these are *free* markets. For example, market socialism does not involve the attachment to private property in free-market accounts. Even if certain centre-left reformers place greater emphasis on markets, they are not necessarily committed to endorsing *free* market proposals. This remains the case even if arguments for free markets were an important factor in explaining why these reformists placed greater weight on markets. Here free markets may be important since it helps create a space within which reformists can examine existing commitments, but from a standpoint informed by centre-left traditions. Martin Smith has applied this perspective in his analysis of the Labour party's Policy Review conducted between 1987 and 1990 (Smith 1992). One of the central themes of this review was an acceptance that markets had to play a greater role in any centre-left account. Smith accepts that the Thatcher governments played an important role in fostering this change. But he contends that reformism did not simply catch up to Thatcherite free markets. Rather Thatcherism was important because it created a space within which reformists could examine their own ideological commitments. Smith argues that this licenses a different conception of both market and state activity, which implies in turn significant institutional differences. This is not to say that Hay will endorse this sort of reformism. He may still regard this as being inferior to his project of reconstructing centre-left reformism around a new state tradition. The nature of his criticism of this alternative reformism now differs in character, however. In particular he asserts the importance of top-down over bottom-up reform, rather than centre-left reformism over catch-up to free markets. It may transpire that the centre-left is ultimately better served by the top-down reformism that Hay endorses rather than the alternative bottom-up approach. To assess this it is important to examine what this alternative reformism amounts to, not what it does not.

Globalisation

Another set of issues impinged on the viability of any reformist strategy. The fall of state socialism in the former USSR and Eastern Europe in the late 1980s and early 1990s had led to doubts being expressed regarding whether any left politics was viable in modern conditions. This view was expressed most famously perhaps in Francis Fukuyama's claim that society was now at the 'end of history'. Here there is no viable alternative to a society based on liberal democracy in the polity and free markets in the economy (Fukuyama 1992). Accordingly, the search for a coherent alternative to both free markets and Keynesian social democracy also had to consider whether this was viable in modern conditions. This principally meant addressing globalisation. Since rising to prominence during the 1990s, there are now few public policy debates that make no reference to globalisation. Globalisation however is a multifaceted concept, and has been deployed in a variety of ways. Its economic dimensions are perhaps most obvious, referring usually to a combination of changes in the volume, and speed, of transactions in global capital markets, an intensification of global trade, the growth in importance of transnational corporations and changes in information and communications technology. Globalisation however is not simply (or, for some, even mainly) an economic phenomenon: it has also been taken to refer to social dimensions encompassing a recasting of spatial–temporal relationships and changes in the nature of risk (Giddens 1999). One feature of importance is the supposed impulse given to the creation of a plural society. This is a society marked by a deep diversity of lifestyles. Although economic globalisation is seen, at times, as a threat to particular identities (through global branding, for example), some thinkers associate globalisation more strongly with pluralism. Globalisation is, for example, understood here to create a space within which traditional roles (between men and women say) may be rethought, resulting in individuals articulating a greater variety of identities. Some have suggested that globalisation makes any sort of reformist project (and, thus, any search for a 'third way') defunct. With respect to means, it is suggested that global economic changes imply that it is more difficult for the state to intervene within the context of the national economy. In some models, the state's capacities have largely withered away. Since centre-left reformers have traditionally relied on state intervention to realise policy goals, these changes for critics have undermined the central mechanism of social democracy. With respect to ends or objectives, it is suggested that centre-left politics is unable to confront plural society adequately. Gray alleges that social democracy is challenged since it is committed to a single vision of the good society, revolving around a commitment to equality.

Liberalism similarly faces difficulties in integrating non-liberal values that emerge from multicultural society (Gray 1997). As well as making it more difficult to construct appeals to individuals with plural identities, it is not clear that centre-left reformers ought to be endorsing such an approach.

A common charge was that globalisation was mandating an acceptance of free-market assumptions. One response to these changes rejects the idea that there has been a qualitative change within the global economy. Paul Hirst and Grahame Thompson for example contend that many of the features taken to define economic globalisation have in fact been present in earlier eras, and possibly in a more extensive form (Hirst and Thompson 1996). They emphasise, accordingly, continuity rather than discontinuity. The death of the nation-state in particular has been exaggerated and the possibility (if not necessarily desirability) of conventional centre-left politics remains. Similarly, it may be contended that the centre-left have always had to accommodate different lifestyles since pluralism is a perennial feature of society. Differences between contemporary and earlier manifestations, on this view, are exaggerated. A second response accepts the importance of qualitative changes in the global economy, but denies that this has undermined the basis for centre-left politics This emphasises that globalisation is not a fixed process, but that it can be shaped and directed through political action (Perraton, Goldblatt, Held and McGrew 1997). Even if global changes have undermined conventional objectives and means deployed within centre-left politics, reformers are free to explore alternatives. Centre-left politics permits experimentation with different forms of political construction. Even if global changes have undermined conventional objectives and means deployed within the centre-left, reformists are free to explore alternatives. With respect to social democracy, for example, this recognises that social democracy,

> is not a fixed doctrine, but a political movement, as protean as the capitalist economy and society which has given rise to it. It is not a particular historical programme or regime or political party or interest group, or even an unchanging set of values. As a political movement its only fixed point is its constant search to build and sustain political majorities for reforms of economic and social institutions which counter injustice and reduce inequality.
> (Gamble and Wright 1999, p. 2)

On this view, although social democracy does not constitute a theory, social democrats can nevertheless draw on and deploy theories. It is possible that different theories may be deployed in different contexts. This is not to say that globalisation leaves the nature of reformism untouched. It has, for example, raised the profile of bottom-up traditions. One of the consequences of globalisation was a greater emphasis on exploring alternative governance arrangements to the state. This analysis of alternative governance arrangements fell largely within the province of bottom-up traditions, thereby raising its profile. If globalisation pointed to greater weight on bottom-up traditions, it also altered the nature of these traditions. Bottom-up analysis had to be reconstructed to respond both to the imperatives posed by the global economy and to the challenges posed by plural society.

Stakeholding

Stakeholding was an attempt to construct an alternative to both free markets and Keynesian social democracy. Its significance lay in this attempt to provide an alternative to the two main frameworks that informed policy since 1945 and which were, for different reasons, seen as unsatisfactory. As Will Hutton noted,

> Britain is not succeeding as it should. The difficulty is not its attachment to capitalism; market principles could hardly have been applied more fiercely over the last seventeen years ... The solution is neither to pursue the current path, nor to attempt any return to the failed corporatism of the 1970s. Rather it is to strike out in a new direction altogether, escaping the polarities of collectivism and individualism through which capitalism has so often been analysed and interpreted, towards a new conception of the stakeholder economy and society.
>
> (Hutton 1997a, p. 1)

Stakeholding was important for reformers since it was seen as a potential way of renewing the centre-left. Two themes dominate this book. First, it is argued that stakeholding constitutes a viable 'third way'. Setting this out has three main dimensions. The first is that stakeholding furnishes a coherent set of principles to inform reforms of public policy. When it first emerged it was unclear whether stakeholding could be fashioned to form a coherent set of public policy principles. Indicative of this was the way in which stakeholding was applied to a variety of different contexts, with little apparent consistency. Surveying these debates, Gavin Kelly, Dominic Kelly and Andrew Gamble noted, 'Almost everything it seems has a stakeholder dimension: stakeholder capitalism, stakeholder government, stakeholder Europe, stakeholder society, stakeholder economy' (Kelly, Kelly and Gamble 1997, p. 238). This suggested that stakeholding might for all its initial appeal prove to be ultimately vacuous. But, as Kelly et al. argue, 'If stakeholding were so vacuous ... it would not have attracted so much attention or stimulated so much controversy' (ibid.). This book contends that stakeholding can in fact be associated with a coherent set of public policy principles. Like many other intricate notions, stakeholding has a number of different facets. It is not a single body of thought but displays variety within, and between, strands. It is not my aim to offer an exhaustive survey of the whole of stakeholder theory, but rather to focus on two central aspects of this for understanding policy. I distinguish between 'collectivist' and 'individualist' accounts. Collectivist stakeholding examines the ways in which collective institutions such as firms and public services are governed and run. Individualist stakeholding concentrates on providing individuals with their own assets or stakes. The collectivist and individualist strands of stakeholding can be constructed in a variety of ways. It is argued here that in Britain these strands are fashioned to promote the individual acquisition of responsibility and knowledge organised around the possession of stakes. Responsibility means that individuals acquire and develop particular virtues, such as trust, cooperation and personal responsibility. Knowledge here is taken to refer to the acquisition of knowledge that yields benefits. Although this includes efficiency benefits, benefits here will not simply be seen in these terms. It will also include, for example, the contribution knowledge can make towards enhancing the choices made by individuals. Though this understanding is not so wide as to admit knowledge that has little benefit, it is not so narrow as to be confined to efficiency benefits.

The focus on responsibility and knowledge overlaps, but is distinct from, issues of citizenship. Theories of citizenship are ethical accounts devoted to the various rights and responsibilities that accrue to all individuals as members of a political community (Faulks 2000). Insofar as stakeholding considers the various rights and responsibilities of individuals in a political community, it overlaps with theories of citizenship. Indeed, some contributors refer to citizenship when discussing stakeholding. Although important, this book concentrates on individual responsibility and knowledge rather than citizenship. This reflects the importance of efficiency dimensions, and is revealed most obviously with respect to knowledge. While the accumulation of skills can be integrated in a theory of citizenship insofar as the exercise of citizenship may require that individuals have to acquire skills, the focus on knowledge acquisition also emerges from separate efficiency considerations. Here stakeholding helps promote efficiency by fostering knowledge acquisition and deployment regardless of any moral theory. Debates regarding inclusion are connected to this. Inclusion relates to the conditions of membership of a political community, and hence to citizenship. Although inclusion is important for various theorists of stakeholding, the efficiency dimension of responsibility and knowledge points beyond a focus on inclusion. The book looks at individual responsibility and skills rather than citizenship since this captures the efficiency dimension alongside any moral commitments.

Discussion of stakeholding will concentrate mainly on the analysis of stakeholding in relation to social democracy. This is not because there is any necessary connection between stakeholding and social democracy. Stakeholding is not the exclusive property of any particular political tradition. As will be seen later, a version of stakeholding appeared on the right in the guise of popular capitalism. If stakeholding is not therefore specific to any single political tradition, accounts of stakeholding nevertheless differed across political traditions. This view recognises that political discussion ultimately shapes frameworks, and that different models emerge from different discussions across political traditions. The book centres on social democracy since this has been the most important site for the discussion of stakeholding in Britain. At an intellectual level, the most developed accounts of stakeholding in Britain were conducted in relation to social democracy. At a political level, the traditional representatives of British social democracy, that is the Labour party and trade unions, expressed greatest interest in stakeholding. The most important context for stakeholding in Britain, accordingly, has been with regard to social democracy. This is not to say that stakeholding was simply an immanent tradition within social democracy, waiting to be discovered. Seeing social democracy as a practice precludes the existence of any immanent framework. Since stakeholding is seen here as a potential framework, this means that stakeholding is not immanent to social democracy.

Secondly, establishing whether stakeholding represents a coherent set of principles of public policy need not imply, however, that it constitutes an alternative both to free markets and Keynesian social democracy. Indeed, this is denied in some quarters. For example, some allege that stakeholding represents a policy of free market catch-up. Josephine Maltby and Roy Wilkinson argue that stakeholding may be 'merely the most sophisticated public relations effort yet mounted on behalf of the free market' (Maltby and Wilkinson 1998, p. 204). The book considers, secondly, the extent to which stakeholding is distinct from both free markets and Keynesian social democracy. This discussion simply aims to establish whether stakeholding is in fact a coherent alternative to the two main frameworks that have dominated post-war British government. It is argued that stakeholding does give substance to the notion of a third way. It is not suggested that stakeholding ought to be the sole basis for a third way. It is possible to generate a range of projects that are separate from both free markets and Keynesian social democracy, one of which is stakeholding. Although stakeholding may be superior to these different accounts, it is also possible that it may be inferior or, at best, an adjunct to a different approach. Though interesting, I do not confront this question here since it is beyond the scope of this book.

A coherent alternative to free markets and Keynesian social democracy might not, however, be viable in contemporary conditions. As such, stakeholding is considered, thirdly, within the context of globalisation, exploring how it confronts the challenges posed by the global economy and society. Some individuals expressed scepticism about the extent of global changes. Will Hutton argued that while 'I accept that the world in which one is trying to build stakeholder capitalism is changing and that internationalisation grows apace, I am also a bit of a sceptic where some of the more extreme claims of some protagonists of the globalisation thesis are concerned' (Hutton 1997b, p. 7). Others placed more weight on such changes. For John Plender earlier forms of stakeholding (associated particularly with German and Japanese models of capitalism) were less relevant within an altered global context. He contended that these models were developed largely within a closed economy framework. By opening up these boundaries, global changes were undermining the foundations of these models. He argued, 'with Japan and Germany both now operating in highly competitive global markets for goods, services and capital, it becomes increasingly difficult for them to sustain uneconomic subsidies at home from one group of stakeholders to another' (Plender 1997, p. 26). Plender argued that it was important to develop new forms of stakeholding, suggesting in fact that a reconstructed stakeholder theory 'seems more relevant to the modern information economy than the unreconstructed shareholder model on which Anglo-Saxon capitalism currently relies' (ibid., p. 3). The book argues that both collectivist and individualist strains of stakeholding are viable in a contemporary context.

New Labour

My second theme highlights the importance of stakeholding for understanding New Labour. Tony Blair's interest in stakeholding in his speech in Singapore is noted above. Stakeholding attracted much attention among other acolytes of New Labour (looked at in greater detail in Chapter 6). It provoked scrutiny since it seemed to form a new public policy agenda that broke free from the 'old Labour' emphasis on the state and public ownership, and the Conservative stress on free markets. New Labour interest in stakeholding provoked a hostile reaction from the right. Conservative politicians suggested that stakeholding simply marked a return to old-style corporatism characterised by high strike activity, spiralling wage demands and poor industrial relations. Brian Mawhinney declared, for example, that stakeholder proposals simply mean that 'Labour's old friends in the trade union movement would get back all the power and privileges that they abused in the 1970s' (quoted in Webster 1996). David Willetts suggested similarly that stakeholding simply showed that Labour was still beholden to trade unions and 'old vested interests, dressed up in the latest language of corporate strategy' (Willetts 1996). Will Hutton noted that when 'Mr Blair invoked stakeholding in his Singapore speech in January 1996, the intensity of the reaction and scale of criticism took both him and the then shadow cabinet by surprise' (Hutton 1999b, p. 268). Hutton claims that although Blair was interested in stakeholding as an overall organising project, he found that 'John Monks liked it and Will

Hutton liked it, so he ran a mile' (Hutton 2000a, p. 56). Although Blair offered some reaction to these criticisms (for example in a speech at Derby on 18 January 1996), he ultimately began to retreat from deploying explicit stakeholder discourse. For Hutton this demonstrated a 'staggering lack of self-confidence, produced by the loss of four successive elections' (ibid., p. 57). On this view, Blair was keen to avoid the criticisms that were directed at old Labour. To avoid these criticisms Blair had an incentive to avoid stakeholder discourse. Stakeholder discourse was superseded by references to the 'third way'.

A common judgement is that New Labour flirted only briefly with stakeholding. Nicholas Huntington and Tim Bale contest that 'in its early days it tried on stakeholding ... [but] it dropped it very quickly' (Huntington and Bale 2002, p. 47). Richard Heffernan argues similarly that 'stakeholding as an idea got no further than the starting block' (Heffernan 2001, p. 23). This book questions this judgement. It is argued, in particular, that a significant part of New Labour policy since being elected to government in 1997 overlaps with stakeholding. It is not denied that New Labour has scaled down its attachment to stakeholding since Blair's speech in Singapore. It does not function as an overall organising project in the way that it was once suggested. Nevertheless it remains an important element of New Labour's approach. It is contested that policy has shown moves in both of the directions implied by these strands of stakeholding. The discussion is important for correcting misperceptions about the significance of stakeholding and for understanding a core part of government policy.

Chapter outlines

Chapter 2 examines the first of two broad strands of stakeholding that attracted attention in Britain, that is, collectivist stakeholding. This approach has its roots in discussions relating to the governance of corporations as well as public services. Will Hutton's *The State We're In* raised the profile of debates surrounding corporate governance. After setting out his account, the chapter examines how his arguments were contested and developed by others. Special attention is paid to the most cogent models that emerged in this tradition, encompassing the approach of contributors such as John Kay and John Plender. Collectivist stakeholding was not confined to examining corporate governance. The chapter considers how stakeholding was applied, at both a theoretical and practical level, to other realms (such as debates about public services). The chapter concludes by pulling together the common themes informing the different agendas. It shows that the central thrust of this looks at how stakeholding can be used to help promote individual responsibility and skills. The ways these themes of responsibility and knowledge support and conflict with each other are explored.

Chapter 3 considers the nature of stakeholder discourse within the second main context of individualist stakeholding. The importance of an early version of stakeholding that was developed on the right, in particular popular capitalism, is noted. Popular capitalism was also significant for the centre-left. The chapter studies how the centre-left constructed its own version of popular capitalism focusing on welfare, with particular attention being paid to policies such as stakeholder pensions and individual learning accounts. More generally, drawing in part from academic writing in the United States, attention is placed on asset-based welfare. As with Chapter 2, the general themes informing different models are set out. It is argued that the stress on individual responsibility and knowledge organised around the possession of stakes links these different models.

Chapter 4 explores the general institutional configuration implied by stakeholding. It is suggested that both collectivist and individualist models place emphasis on a combination of markets and civil society. The nature, as well as the particular combination, of markets and civil society in collectivist and individualist accounts is considered. The above emphasis does not imply that there is no important role for the state, and the state's role in collectivist and individualist accounts is examined. The chapter also scrutinises the nature of a particularly important type of stake, namely ownership. Two different agendas for promoting responsibility and knowledge are identified. A distributive agenda focuses on spreading individual property ownership. A hybrid agenda examines the mix between the rights and responsibilities of property. The relationship of these ownership agendas and collectivist and individualist approaches is contemplated.

Chapter 5 considers criticisms of a stakeholder agenda. Stakeholding faced a host of critiques when it first emerged. Some alleged it was incoherent. Others claimed that it did not break with the policies previously adopted by either Labour or the Conservatives. Still others said that it could not be made to work in modern circumstances. Though distinct, each of these criticisms denies the importance of stakeholding as a new and interesting way of looking at public policy. The chapter challenges these criticisms arguing that stakeholding is a more subtle and robust set of ideas than many of its detractors contended. Many of these critics did not concentrate their fire on the strongest accounts of stakeholding. This chapter shows that their critiques would have been answered if they had. Stakeholding, in both collectivist and individualist guises, is not an incoherent set of ideas, but points instead to a set of principles that break from old politics and are feasible in modern circumstances. This underlines that stakeholding is an interesting perspective in public policy and is worthy of further development. The differences between recent attempts on the left and right to chart other third ways are recorded, to show the distinctiveness of the stakeholder position. The chapter also studies the way in which collectivist and individualist versions of stakeholding overlap. Although it is useful for analytical reasons to separate out different strands of stakeholding, the way they were constructed in Britain shows important overlaps. The chapter reflects on the way in which they are combined, as well as tensions that arise from this.

Chapter 6 sets out the importance of stakeholding for New Labour. It underlines the important role stakeholding plays in New Labour thinking. Although explicit references to stakeholding were scaled down, it is still significant for understanding the driving forces behind New Labour thought. The importance of stakeholder arguments is clear in the writings and speeches of Tony Blair, Anthony Giddens and Peter Mandelson, and this remains an important part of third-way discussions. The chapter also sets out the importance of stakeholding for New Labour's actual policy record. Part of this looks at moves in stakeholder directions in policy towards corporations, focusing for instance on the deliberations of the Company Law Review. This is complemented by a study of welfare reform, showing that policies on welfare-to-work, stakeholder pensions, individual learning accounts and capital grants all demonstrate significant stakeholder elements. It shows how this agenda is being consolidated and expanded in New Labour's second term. Chapter 6 is followed by a conclusion that provides a summary of the arguments of the book as well as a set of brief reflections.

2
Collectivist Stakeholding

Centre-left politics, as noted in Chapter 1, was forced onto the defensive for much of the 1980s. Arguments from the right succeeded in shaking the beliefs of many reformers. One of the hallmarks of progressive politics is an attachment to collective institutions. For much of the twentieth century, this was manifested in a reliance on the state. As a result of New Right critiques, however, many on the centre-left accepted the limitations of the state. But reformists were unhappy with free-market prescriptions. Attention was devoted to developing models of collective intervention that did not simply rely on the state. Stakeholding was at the forefront of this attempt to create a new collectivist agenda for the left, which concerned, in particular, collectivist models of stakeholding. This strand of stakeholding focuses on two main realms. First, the ways in which businesses are organised and run. Second, the way in which stakeholder principles can be applied more broadly to the realm between the individual and the state (which encompasses 'civil society'). An important component of this studies how public services are organised and run. As noted above, collectivism historically has had strong associations with state intervention. The term will be used here to refer to forms of collective organisation, including the study of corporations. As the examination of companies has not usually been seen as a species of collectivism, this means that the sense in which I use collectivism in this book does not necessarily have traditional connotations. This chapter considers the assumptions underpinning the different dimensions of collectivist stakeholding, demonstrating that a coherent set of principles informs the way in which collectivist accounts of stakeholding have been constructed in Britain. This focuses centrally on how institutions can be organised to promote individual responsibility and knowledge.

Background

The first main component of collectivist models looks at the governance of corporations. Much of the relevant frame of reference was identified by Adolf Berle and Gardiner Means during the 1930s. Berle and Means argued that a fundamental transformation in corporate governance was occurring. In the past, those who provided the financial capital for a firm (and by virtue of this were the owners of the firm) were the individuals who also exercised management over the firm's resources. This tradition of owner-management was being radically altered according to Berle and Means in the modern corporation. In particular the growth in size of the modern corporation meant that those who owned shares in a firm were no longer the same people who ran the corporation. For Berle and Means this separation of ownership from control had given rise to passive ownership. Part of this resulted from informational considerations. Separation of ownership and control meant individual shareholders faced information problems in monitoring managers. Managers were not only relatively better informed about their personal and company performance, they could also manipulate the information passed on to the shareholders. Incentive problems ran alongside this. Since the benefits of a shareholder intervention were spread across all shareholders, while the cost of an intervention was borne solely by the intervening shareholder, there was an individual incentive to free-ride on others. In some cases, this might mean that monitoring would not occur at all. Here underperforming managers would be unpunished for underperformance.

Berle and Means trace three basic responses to this state of affairs. One was to maintain the status quo and insist that the corporation still belonged to its shareholders. Company law should ensure that managers operate the 'corporation for the *sole* benefit of the security owners' (Berle and Means 1932, p. 354). This in fact defines the treatment of the firm in orthodox economic analysis, and is often referred to as the shareholder model of the firm. Shareholders here are owners of the firm; they delegate daily running of the firm to a set of managers or an agent. Typically there is a conflict of interests between managers and shareholders. It is usually assumed that shareholders are interested in the maximisation of profits. Managers in contrast aim to maximise their personal happiness, which is assumed to diverge from shareholder objectives. This conflict of interests gives rise to the problem of how shareholders can motivate managers to act in shareholder interests. Examining strategies for alleviating this is a central preoccupation of orthodox theory, which concentrates on how contracts can be written to ensure that managers have an incentive to further shareholder objectives. Shareholders, for example, could offer managers a pay package that includes a component that is tied to the profitability of a firm. This means that the greater the profits, the greater their pay. This provides an incentive, accordingly, for directors to maximise profits (Hart 1995). But the problem with this for Berle and Means was that passive ownership meant that shareholders no longer exercised the responsibilities corresponding to their rights. As such, if the conventional view of ownership was strengthened, 'the bulk of American industry might soon be operated by trustees for the sole benefit of inactive and irresponsible security owners' (Berle and Means 1932, p. 354). A second view would be to invest ownership simply with the firm's managers. On this view, 'corporate development has created a new set of relationships, giving to the groups in control powers which are absolute and not limited by any implied obligation with respect to their use' (ibid.). This for them would lead to the danger of 'corporate oligarchy with the probability of an era of corporate plundering' (ibid., p. 353). Beyond these two approaches, a third strategy is advocated. In particular,

> [changes have placed] the community in a position to demand that the modern corporation serve not alone the owners or the control, but all society. The third alternative offers a wholly new concept of corporate activity ... When a convincing system of community obligations is worked out and is generally accepted, in that the passive property of today must yield before the larger interests of society'.
>
> (Ibid., pp. 355–6)

Corporate governance stakeholding

Corporate governance stakeholding arose largely within the context of this third tradition. Kevin Keasey, Steve Thompson and Mike Wright argue, 'the central proposition at the heart of the stakeholder approach is that the purpose – the objective function – of the firm should be defined more widely than the maximization of shareholder welfare alone' (Keasey et al. 1997, p. 8). In essence this captures the view that although managers have responsibilities towards those who supply financial capital to the firm, they also have responsibilities towards a wider set of stakeholders. These stakeholders encompass consumers, members of the local community and firm suppliers. This general approach covers a range of different, and sometimes opposing, strategies. One strand focuses on stakeholding as a moral idea. This was important for Swedish management theorist Eric Rhenman, one of the first to refer explicitly to stakeholder corporate governance. For Rhenman,

> stakeholders ... designate the individuals or groups which depend on the company for the realisation of their personal goals and on whom the company is dependent. In this sense employees, owners, customers, suppliers and creditors as well as many other groups can all be regarded as stakeholders in the company. (Rhenman 1967, p. 25)

Rhenman argued that this view of the firm supported industrial democracy. This involved spreading democratic practices throughout a firm. It was seen as the best way of reconciling the differing claims of the various stakeholder groups that make up a firm into a common unity. Industrial democracy must 'try to contribute to the development of the best possible methods and institutions for resolving conflicts and establishing co-operation' (ibid., p. 122). Another strand is rooted more closely in efficiency considerations. This tradition emphasises that negotiation with stakeholders is central for the attainment of profits. One important theme here understands stakeholding as a type of corporate strategy, intended to boost profits, and was important for researchers such as Otis J. Benepe and Robert F. Stewart at the Stanford Research Institute in California during the 1960s through to later theorists such as Richard Freeman (Freeman 1984).

The state we're in

When it first emerged within Britain, stakeholding became quickly associated with Will Hutton's approach. Some indication of this is given by the fact that when criticisms of stakeholding were expressed, these were usually directed against Hutton's model. Two central themes informed Hutton's analysis. First an economic component, which suggested that

> the weakness of the British economy, particularly the level and character of investment, originates in the financial system. The targets for profit are too high and time horizons are too short. But British finance has not grown up in a vacuum. Behind the financial institutions stand history, class, a set of values and the political system. The City of London and Whitehall and Westminster are symbiotic; one could not exist without the other, and none could have become what they are today without the others' support.
>
> (Hutton 1996a, p. xxvii)

Discipline on managers within British corporations is expressed for Hutton via financial markets. Here, ready exit opportunities allow shareholders to sell their shares quickly if incumbent managers are underperforming. This may lead to a takeover which, if realised, is likely to see the installation of new managers. Although intended to promote efficiency, Hutton argues the effect is the reverse. Under the pressure of possible shareholder exit, managers are forced to divert resources from any long-term investments to pay out high short-term dividends. This 'short-termism' is problematic for Hutton, since these long-term investments are often central to a firm's success. Ewart Keep and Ken Mayhew argue that Hutton analyses British capitalism as a 'system' composed of interlocking parts; that for Hutton the British system is suboptimal in efficiency terms, exhibiting, as a result, 'systems failure' (Keep and Mayhew 1998). A political thesis, secondly, ran alongside this. Here the 'semi-modern nature of the British state is a fundamental cause of Britain's economic and social problems' (Hutton 1996 pp. xxvii–xxviii). Colin Hay argues that Hutton draws here on Perry Anderson's analysis of the peculiar nature of the historical development of British capitalism. Anderson argued that although Britain was the first nation to industrialise, many of the pre-industrial institutions remained intact. A bourgeois class was never fully formed and there was, accordingly, an incomplete bourgeois revolution. This affected the nature of further capitalist development. This prevented the emergence of a modern state which was needed to secure efficiency in a modern economy

(Anderson 1964; Hay 1996). Markets are embedded in a series of social and political institutions for Hutton, but these are of a semi-modern nature in Britain's case. Accordingly, constitutional reform is required, and this has a variety of facets. One feature is introducing a written constitution (which encompasses a bill of rights). Another is a focus on shifting power away from central government. This includes steps towards federalism as well as a measure of regional devolution.

Criticisms of Hutton

Hutton's approach attracted a variety of criticisms. Some objected to specific claims he made regarding British capitalism. Tim Congdon argues that there is little evidence of high returns on capital in the UK. Returns merely reflect Western European averages (Congdon 1997). Meghnad Desai maintains that the problem with British capitalism is not the performance of the financial sector (which is a strength) but poor profitability in the manufacturing sector (Desai 1997). Hutton's account of short-termism was also susceptible to the criticism that even if managers and shareholders possess different time horizons, this may not matter if financial intermediation allows the separation of these different time horizons. Many of these criticisms were accepted by, and indeed some originated from, other centre-left theorists who contributed to stakeholding. John Kay notes,

> as is now generally recognized, the arguments which are commonly formulated in the attack on short-termism are wrong... [these] fail to appreciate the central role which financial intermediation has, and achieves successfully: a divorce between the time horizons of borrowers and the time horizons of lenders. (Kay 1994a, p. 63)

Kay argues that this model of short-termism is flawed. He argues that even if shareholders prefer shorter investment projects than managers do, the nature of financial markets means that managers are insulated from shareholder demands. Rather than having to raise funds to pay for investment projects by issuing equity or shares (and so be subject to shareholder pressure), managers can circumvent this by borrowing from financial markets (where such pressures are absent). The nature of financial markets means that managers do not have to turn to shareholders to finance projects. In any case, it is not clear why shareholders should be hostile to long-term projects if they increased overall profitability. Gerald Holtham, referring to *The State We're In*, argued 'many of the links ... in his *tour de force* are questionable. The evidence is mixed and not compelling' (Holtham 1997, p. 3). John Plender suggested that Hutton's association with stakeholding helped contribute to stakeholding's fall from grace in public discussions. He argued that under 'the unwitting influence of this engaging and enthusiastic advocate, the Big Idea suddenly started to shrink' (Plender 1997, p. 14).

Stakeholder alternatives

Rather than dispense with stakeholding altogether, theorists sought to develop an alternative understanding of stakeholding. Here I concentrate on an account that confines, as John Parkinson notes, the 'term "stakeholder" to those who enter long-term cooperative relationships with the company' (Parkinson 1997a, p. 149). Here, it 'is not customers and suppliers as generalised groups who are stakeholders, but individual members of these groups' (ibid., p. 150). In his model Parkinson explores how company law can be used to foster cooperative relationships. Although Parkinson accepts that the existing legal framework allows managers to engage in cooperative relationships, he holds that this should be made more explicit. One key instrument for this is the reformulation of directors' duties to take more explicit account developing relationships with stakeholders (see Box 2.1 below for examples of key reforms advocated by supporters of corporate governance stakeholding). Parkinson also considered the importance of instituting a two-tier board, the first managerial tier complemented by a second tier containing representatives of various stakeholders (Parkinson 1997b). I concentrate on the latter, since this was the most coherent and robust model of stakeholding developed within the context of corporate governance. One of the most cogent models here was developed by the economist and management theorist John Kay (Kay 1997a; 1997b; 1997c; 1996a; 1996b; 1996c; 1994a; 1994b; 1994c; 1993). Kay's importance was recognised by others who contributed to stakeholding. For example Gerald Holtham contended that Kay developed the strongest account of stakeholder corporate governance (Holtham 1997).

As well as collaborating with Kay on his early work, Holtham was important in policy discussions given his role as director of the left-leaning think-tank the Institute for Public Policy Research during the mid-1990s (the IPPR was set up in 1988 with the support of politicians such as the then leader of the Labour party Neil Kinnock and Theresa Blackstone to provide public policy research and advice for the centre-left). Although Kay collaborated with Hutton at times, Kay's own account accommodates many of the important criticisms directed at Hutton's approach. Although there were other accounts of stakeholding, I concentrate on Kay since he developed one of the most cogent models within the context of corporate governance.

Opportunism and cooperation

Considering the costs imposed by opportunism is a starting point for understanding this version of stakeholding, Holtham and Kay argue,

> Unbridled individualism is not only not the same as capitalism; it is actually inimical to capitalism. The most individualist of market societies of market economies is not the United States; it is Nigeria, where the expectation of opportunistic behaviour is so universal that economic life is effectively crippled.
>
> (Holtham and Kay 1994, pp. 2–3)

For Holtham and Kay, costs imposed by opportunism can be so severe as to undermine the basis of economic activity. Opportunistic behaviour is costly for these thinkers because it increases the transaction costs of economic activity. Oliver Williamson argued that transaction cost problems arise with the conjunction of three conditions (Williamson 1985). First, the existence of uncertainty surrounding economic transactions. This means that it is not possible to define economic transactions in a set of fully explicit contracts. Second, 'asset specificity'. That is any investments made in an economic transaction are such that the value of switching elsewhere will in general yield less value for transacting parties than remaining within the existing transaction. Lastly, a behavioural assumption that suggests that all economic actors are opportunistic and motivated by self-interest and guile. Employee 'hold-up' is an example of a transaction cost problem. This looks at an employee decision about whether or not to invest in a training course that would benefit their employer. The managers of a firm may promise the worker that they will raise their wage if the worker engages in training. Employers may be reluctant, however, to specify the precise nature of the increase because they say that this depends in part on future economic conditions that they cannot predict with certainty (the state of consumer demand, the interest rates they have to pay on any outstanding loans and so on). This points to the existence of the first feature required for a transaction cost, namely, the existence of uncertainty. The second aspect is fulfilled if it is not easy for a worker to transfer the skills learnt elsewhere (so there is asset-specificity). The transaction cost arises with the conjunction of the third condition, that is, managerial opportunism. In particular, once a worker has paid for training, an employer may behave opportunistically and renege on the promise to reward the investment in an appropriate fashion. At this point the worker is 'held up'. The employee cannot force the employer to honour their commitment properly (since there is no contract). Moreover, the worker cannot recoup the cost of training by moving elsewhere (since the skills acquired are specific to the practices of their present employer). As employees are aware of most of the above before making their decision, they are unlikely to pay for training (even though the individual and firm would benefit from this training). This transaction cost leads to departures from the efficient level of investment. Reducing transaction costs implies deviating from at least one of the above conditions. For example, without asset specificity agents could always switch to equally profitable outside options should any problems emerge, without loss. In relation to employee hold-up, this means that workers gain general skills that can be easily applied in other firms.

Transaction cost economics is important for understanding many of the models of corporate governance stakeholding. For Holtham and Kay, most economic activity is characterised by uncertainty. Given that an important part of any investments made within a firm displays specificity (such as investments in specific skills required by a firm), the existence of opportunism means the manifestation, following Williamson, of transaction cost problems. To mitigate such costs, these thinkers focus particularly on deviating from opportunism: the theorists aim to depart from opportunism by promoting cooperation. In doing so efficiency is enhanced, which in the context of firms means promoting profits. This is the basis of Kay's reformulation of a 'short-termism' critique. Although Kay accepted the central flaw in standard views of 'short-termism',

> exposing this clear technical fallacy has not made the short-termism/long-termism argument die ... [my] arguments here are designed to explain why there may, indeed, be something in it. The development of an environment in which organizational knowledge can be created and a co-operative ethic established requires an assurance of long-term relationships ... which is hostile to opportunistic behaviour.
>
> (Kay 1994a, p. 63)

Cooperation is inculcated through 'architecture'. This is 'a structure which achieves the growth of organizational knowledge, or the development of a co-operative ethic' (ibid., p. 59). Architecture is said to have internal and external dimensions: internally it refers to structures within a firm, externally to structures between a firm and outside parties. Architecture helps promote a cooperative ethic essentially through a two-step process. First, architecture maps out an institutional context supportive of regular interaction between individuals over time. These are 'long-term' interactions. Mutual interaction helps, secondly, to develop mutual bonds such as cooperation. Although the evolution of cooperation is not guaranteed (mutual interaction may be antagonistic, for example), for Kay architecture nevertheless constitutes an important mechanism in practice for the formation of such ties. The connection between long-termism and cooperation is that architecture helps engender cooperation through constructing appropriate repeated games. As he says, the relationships between individuals are 'activities with "Prisoner's Dilemma" properties and are best resolved in a context in which players see themselves as participants in a repeated game, with well-understood strategies for repeated play' (ibid., p. 60). Kay alludes here to the importance of the Prisoner's Dilemma (see Box 2.1). This helps one to understand Kay's criticisms of relying simply on market mechanisms within corporations. By stressing exit from, rather than commitment to, relationships, markets constitute 'short-term' relations inimical to the evolution of cooperation.

Knowledge

This is not to say, however, that Kay simply develops a game theory account. He goes beyond game theory by focusing on the social

Box 2.1 The Prisoner's Dilemma

In the Prisoner's Dilemma the two players are partners who are interviewed separately by the police about a crime they committed. Each prisoner has to decide whether to confess or not confess to the crime. If both players confess, they will receive 3 years in prison each. If both do not confess, they will be convicted on a lesser charge and receive 1 year in prison. If one player confesses, but the other does not confess, the confessor gets freed and the non-confessor gets 5 years (leniency is shown to the confessor for providing sufficient evidence to convict). There is only one play of the game, and both players move simultaneously. All of this information is common knowledge between players. Individuals seek to minimise their time in prison. It is individually better for each individual to confess whatever the strategy of the other player. The case where both confess is an equilibrium. However if both players were able to co-ordinate and agree not to confess, they would both be better off and this would constitute a superior equilibrium. It is not individually rational to do this, thus the individual rational strategy leads to a collectively suboptimal outcome (Varian 1990). When the game is played only once, the best strategy for individuals is to confess rather than not confess. It is possible, however, that repeated play of the game (manifested by each prisoner facing a series of charges) can help generate non-confession. One account of this draws from Robert Axelrod's 'tournaments' (Axelrod 1984). By simulating the effects of different strategies on computers, he found that the best strategy was a 'friendly tit-for-tat' strategy. That is, a person begins by adopting the 'friendly' non-confessing strategy, and continues with this while it is reciprocated by the other person, but in the face of confession, effects a punishment strategy by responding in a tit-for-fat fashion. This helps furnish the evolution of non-confession.

Diagrammatic representation

		Prisoner 2: Confess	Prisoner 2: Do not confess
Prisoner 1	Confess	3, 3	0, 5
	Do not confess	5, 0	1, 1

The first and second number in each cell represents the respective pay-offs of Prisoners 1 and 2.

context within which individuals interact. This is seen in his analysis of business. He agrees with management theorist R. C. Solomon in regarding business as a practice (Kay 1997a). Business for Solomon is a practice, which 'is to say that it is not only a social activity with (at least) several participants but that it has goals and rules and boundaries and a purpose' (Solomon 1992, p. 119). In order to fit into a practice, individuals have to acquire particular virtues. With respect to firms, virtue recognises that 'an employee or executive develops his or her identity largely through the organizations in which he or she spends most of adult working life' (ibid., p. 161). Kay distinguishes between two main ways, or modes, that a business may conduct its affairs, either instrumentally or as a profession. A profession mode views business as comprising a distinct set of standards and values. These values result from business practices. In contrast the instrumental approach views profits as the supreme end. For Solomon, corporate virtues include initiative, honesty and cooperation. This is combined with a focus on knowledge. For Kay, this emphasis is in fact connected to the role played by a cooperative ethos. Cooperation helps sustain a process of learning amongst individuals, as they exchange ideas, learn through trial and error, develop firm-specific skills and so on. Kay suggests that knowledge has an organisational dimension, given that the participation of individuals in ongoing relationships endows these relationships with various collective possibilities. These lead to established practices, which are an asset for firms. Here businesses 'are defined by a nexus of long-established trust relationships... for most successful companies, their history is a principal asset rather than a liability' (Kay 1997a, p. 135). The focus therefore is on fostering cooperation and knowledge. The institutional context, in particular the architecture of firms, is important for fostering this.

Kay advocates a series of reforms to promote stakeholding within firms. Two important proposals refer to the use of managerial statutes as well as the representation of stakeholders on company boards (John Parkinson adopts a similar position in his proposals for reform noted above). Kay supports the idea, first, that managers should have their duties to stakeholders explicitly spelt out. In particular, directors should abide by a charter that sets out their responsibilities to appropriate stakeholders (these cover, for example, provisions related to environmental protection, employee training and quality of service to consumers) (Kay 1997a). To foster accountability directors have to report at regular intervals on the steps they have taken to honour their commitments. Kay advocates, secondly, institutional reforms to the governance structure of firms. One initiative that is touted is altering governance structures so that they allow for some form of stakeholder representation. Stakeholders then have an input into the managerial decision-making process by voicing their concerns. As an example of this Kay says that consumers could be given a place on the boards of utilities such as water. This would help ensure that managers respond more closely to consumer concerns (Kay 1996c).

Another policy proposal that attracts attention concerns measures to spread employee share-ownership beyond those that supply financial capital to a firm. This is seen in the *Financial Times* journalist and commentator John Plender's account of stakeholder corporate governance. His importance as a significant contributor to stakeholder theory is buttressed at a policy level by his membership of the Steering Committee on New Labour's Company Law Review which is considering changes to the legal framework structuring corporate governance. The importance of cooperation is seen in the importance Plender attaches to Robert Putnam's account of social capital (Putnam 2000; Putnam et al. 1993). For Putnam social capital refers 'to features of social organization, such as trust, norms and networks, that can improve the efficiency of society by facilitating co-ordinated actions' (Putnam et al. 1993, p. 167). Putnam uses repeated game theory to analyse the evolution, generally, of cooperation, which promotes efficiency by avoiding coordination failures. For Plender, setting out obligations helps foster responsibility. An important mechanism for doing this relates to individual ownership. Within the context of a firm, this involves spreading individual ownership stakes such as employee share-options. Although rights are important for incentive reasons, Plender argues, stressing only rights helps foster unbridled individualism. Referring to opportunism he claims that: 'heavy emphasis on the exercise of private property rights greatly increases such transactions costs' (Plender 1997, p. 24). By setting obligations as well as the rights of property Plender aims to foster responsible individualism. He draws particular attention to the role of cooperation in helping to reduce 'hold-up' problems. Cooperation by reducing the likelihood of opportunism helps reduce the probability of hold-up problems and so helps foster efficient skills acquisition.

Efficiency

Emphasis on cooperation does not imply that a focus on competition is regarded as unimportant. This emphasis springs largely from recognition that concentrating simply on cooperation is unlikely always to promote economic efficiency. For example, coordination failures, which provide a basic efficiency rationale for cooperation, may not affect all areas of economic activity. Efficiency may be best served here by competition. Cooperation and competition may be reconciled in various ways within stakeholding. While a stake may help define a particular relation of commitment, and help underpin cooperation, there may still be scope for individuals to compete within the broad confines of this relationship. For example, while employees may be granted share ownership stakes, there may still be various incentive schemes within the firm that differentially reward employees for differences in individual productivity, training and so on.

The focus on cooperation and knowledge is intended to promote efficiency. For Plender stakeholding aims to preserve 'human and social capital in the interests of competitive advantage' (Plender 1997, p. 256). Cooperation helps reduce transaction costs and so promotes efficiency, and furthermore permits the efficient acquisition and deployment of skills, which is important for Plender since skills and knowledge are seen as an increasingly important determinant of future competitive advantage. Indeed, some suggest that knowledge is the critical determinant of future economic success (Reich 1992). For Kay, the direct search for company profits is often self-defeating. Using an analogy, he says that we expect a good doctor to

> at least weigh the interests of his patients against his own, if not put them ahead. The curious commercial implication of this is that a doctor whose primary motivation was to increase his income would not be perceived as a good doctor and would be unlikely to succeed even in maximising his income. Doctors who do not aim to maximise revenues may expect to earn more than those who do... [the] commercial analogy follows directly.
> (Kay 1997a, pp. 132–3)

According to Kay, managers ought to focus on generating cooperation from stakeholders and in doing so, through a reduction in transaction costs and the development of knowledge capacities, this will actually maximise profits.

Box 2.2 Examples of key stakeholder reforms of corporate governance

- *Stakeholder representation on company boards*

Stakeholders are given representation on company boards. They can discuss company policy (such as investment choices and pricing strategies) and perhaps have some role in decision-making (by voting on certain initiatives). Examples include John Kay's support for representing consumers within utilities such as water (Kay 1996c) as well as John Parkinson's view that stakeholders such as employees should be represented on two-tier boards.

(Parkinson 1997b)

- *Stakeholder statutes*

The duties of managers to stakeholders are written down in a company statute that they must abide by. This conceives of managers as 'trustees' of a firm's broad mission to stakeholders such as shareholders, employees, members of the local community, and supplier chains (Parkinson 1997a). These measures are often accompanied by disclosure measures. Here managers have to report regularly on how they have fulfilled their objectives set out in the stakeholder statute.

- *Spreading ownership stakes*

Attention is paid to spreading shares beyond those that give financial capital to a firm. This looks, for example, at how employee-share ownership can be used to help generate the commitment of workers to a firm.

(Plender 1997)

Mutual ties

The above discussion considers a special type of collective body. It looks, specifically, at those collective institutions that produce and sell goods or services within the marketplace. The principles outlined above need not only be confined, however, to those organisations that happen to interact within the marketplace. They can also be applied elsewhere. One of the themes of discussions of collectivist stakeholding in Britain looks at how these ideas can be applied to other realms. Part of this is embedded in debates on how this can be used to update social democratic thinking. David Marquand offers an important account of this. He argues,

> Markets are social constructs, embedded in societies, shaped by societies and sustained by societies. The unregulated free market

> which has been the holy grail of British government for fifteen years is a chimera. All markets are regulated – if not by the state, then by custom, convention and the institutions of civil society. (Marquand 1996).

Rather than spontaneously emerging natural orders, Marquand holds that markets are necessarily constituted and defined by societies in which they are located. Given that societies vary across space and time, this means that there are differing conceptions of market activity depending upon the particular social context.

Social construction, for Marquand, rests on ties of mutual obligation. These concern the rules that people owe each other. He argues that this is the enduring legacy of 'ethical socialism'. This sees socialism not as an economic or historical theory, but in terms of a set of moral or ethical ideas. He writes, nothing 'has happened to invalidate the socialist ethic ... all societies, even capitalist ones depend on ties of mutual obligation' (Marquand 1997, p. 69). Mutual obligation is important since it is only through respecting social norms and conventions that social constructions can remain stable. Marquand argues, however, that mutual obligation goes beyond a focus on self-interest, since it involves individuals recognising the interests of others. This does not mean that self-interest is unimportant, only that it is not all-important. This is an important dimension to his criticisms of free-market individualism. It does not mean however that no ties of mutual obligation existed during Thatcherism; indeed Crewe points out the existence of a collectivist ethic among the population. Marquand, however, believes these ties to have been made external to Thatcherism, and in particular were rooted in solidarities forged during the Second World War. With generational change, however, these bonds would fade, and renewing them implies going beyond the assumptions underpinning Thatcherism.

The fading of these bonds would also, for Marquand, reveal problems for social democrats. In particular, the fact that common bonds were generated largely through special historical circumstances diverted social democrats from the fact that, like Thatcherites, albeit for different reasons, they had not generally fostered an adequate environment for the formation of ties of mutual obligation. With the passing of these special historical circumstances, Marquand holds that this problem has become more apparent. The main reason for this, he argues, is linked to the dominant way in which policy was conducted in social democracy. In particular, this predominantly involved top-down implementation, with policy simply imposed by the centre upon individuals. Marquand contends that this focus on top-down processes was in large part a product of assumptions made about individuals. It was generally supposed that individuals were less informed and were more likely to be driven by self-interest than their political masters. The implication of these arguments was that policy ought to be imposed by the centre upon individuals. For Marquand, the assumptions inherent in the top-down tradition were flawed. On the one hand this downplayed problems associated with political elites. Following Hayek, it was not clear whether the centre could ever be as well informed as individuals, and beyond this, the public choice school of thought highlighted the fact that political elites were just as susceptible to self-interest. On the other hand, and more fundamentally, Marquand maintains, policy could only be secured with the active engagement of individuals; people needed ultimately to be persuaded if policy was to develop firm roots. This in turn involved recognising the more realistic view that individuals are capable of growing, and able both to have access to the information required for optimal decisions as well as being driven by mutual obligation instead of self-interest. This conception also provides one resolution to a paradox of Thatcherism: that is, while it posed an effective challenge to various institutions of post-war social democracy it did not, following Crewe, eradicate a collectivist ethic amongst the population. Although individuals, following Marquand, developed ties of mutual obligation, they never formed firm attachments to many of the institutions of post-war social democracy. As such, many of these institutions acquired only shallow roots in society and were challenged effectively by Thatcherism.

Mutual education

This does mean however that according to Marquand social democracy is doomed to failure. There is an alternative bottom-up tradition focusing on participatory policy mechanisms. This pointed for Marquand ultimately to an updated form of social democracy organised around civic republicanism. Civic republicanism is a philosophy that looks at how individuals participate in civic or public arenas in ways dedicated to the common good. Having its roots in classical Greece and Rome, individuals temper a concern with their own private interests with activity designed to promote the good of the community. Attention is paid to involving individuals in the running of the polity, encompassing, for example, dialogue over issues of public concern. Civic republicanism does not insist on a complete submergence of the individual into the collective, because one's good is viewed as a part of the good of the republic. One should not pursue one's good at the expense of the good of other people. Marquand notes of civic republicanism that,

> Particularly resonant are its stress on growth, activity, learning and mutuality: its picture of the self as something that is shaped through constant interaction with other selves is a common and testing endeavour ... the central message of civic republicanism is that the self can develop its full potential and learn how properly to discharge its obligations to other selves only through action in the public realm of a free city.
>
> (Marquand 1997, p. 51)

This concern with civic republicanism is manifested more specifically in a focus on a politics of mutual education. Mutual education combines an emphasis upon knowledge and responsibility. In particular mutual *education* points to knowledge dimensions, while *mutual* education points to a particular model of learning, where individuals are best able to learn in a setting that emphasises interaction with other selves. One strand to Marquand's emphasis is based on a model of human fallibility. By engaging with the arguments of others, individuals may develop better justifications for their own arguments if broadly correct, and altering them appropriately if not. Another strand focuses on the limited abilities of individuals to comprehend the world. In such a situation experimentation and with alternative lifestyles is beneficial for revealing useful information.

Civic republicanism, however, 'is valid, though only after translation into a modern idiom' (ibid.). Pluralism provides one of the main reasons why this would have to be updated. Here the 'common culture that early pluralists took for granted no longer exists ... In the multi-ethnic society we now inhabit, a new common culture would have to be based on something wider than the Judeo-Christian tradition' (Marquand 1998b, p. 8). Although pluralism has always been a feature of society, in the sense of individuals pursuing different types of lifestyle, in previous times many pluralists built their thought upon a shared moral inheritance. This drew importantly from a shared inheritance of Christian or Jewish teaching. Many differences that did emerge existed within the broad parameters set by such teaching. Now such a shared moral inheritance has passed. The emergence of different faiths such as Hinduism, Sikhism, Islam, Buddhism and so on has deepened the pluralism that exists in society. Getting people involved in a project to promote the 'common good' is more difficult to achieve in an era marked by such differences. While civic republican ideals may still be relevant, their assumptions need updating to cope with this new context.

Pluralism

In Marquand's view, stakeholding is an important mechanism for supporting this politics of mutual education within the context of a pluralistic society. This stakeholder agenda is significant, first, because it can help sustain a politics of mutual education. Stakeholding is of importance since it is one of the main ways in which the recognition of others can be institutionalised. It is important, secondly, within the context of pluralistic society. For civic republicans part of the good life is the good that is common to all citizens. These aspects are captured in common institutions. In a plural society, however, the good life goes beyond this and points to the importance of plural goods. These are embodied in local institutions. By fostering local institutions, stakeholding helps contribute to the realisation of such plural goods. That is not to say that this is without problems. One issue raised by pluralism relates to those situations in which it is not possible to compare values according to a common standard. Here, individuals have different conceptions of the good life that cannot be rationally compared. In itself this does not cause problems if the values and institutions that embody these conceptions of the good life can coexist with each other. However problems arise when these conceptions are found to be incompatible with each other. One response is to exclude certain values to guarantee compatibility. Though this may constitute a pragmatic solution, on a moral level the decision to exclude certain values will be arbitrary. A different response that allows the existence of different values, but focuses on mutual accommodation is likely to be preferable. This option implies a politics of compromise. It does not try to generate agreement over values, but agreement that those who adhere to different values will have to modify their claims to accommodate each other. This implies an important role for discussion. Various problems may nevertheless be raised. The terms of any compromise may not be evenly distributed. The burden of any compromise, in particular, may be felt more by minorities since they are likely to face a more difficult task in persuading an opposing majority to moderate their concerns. Protection of minorities here is likely to require going beyond a focus on discussion. A further problem is that some individuals may refuse to enter into discussions with others who hold different values. Indeed, it may be the mark of some values to reject the validity of differing views. In these circumstances conflict is likely to continue until certain values are driven out, or an external settlement is imposed. Without consent any external settlement is unlikely, however, to be stable. As such, discussion is likely to be best placed to resolve incompatibilities, although the existence of the above qualifications highlights its limitations.

Policy commissions

Themes connected to collectivist stakeholding can also be detected in the proposals of significant centre-left policy commissions. An important instance of this is seen in the recommendations of the report of the Commission on Social Justice. The Commission was established under the auspices of the Institute for Public Policy Research after Labour's fourth consecutive general election defeat in 1992.[1] This was at the instigation of John Smith, who suggested it during his successful leadership campaign. The Commission was charged with examining and developing centre-left strategies for social justice, and economic efficiency suitable for modern conditions. The Commission formed an important part of policy reform in a sustained period since the 1980s. This reform was inspired by the perception that policy failures (especially around the early 1980s) had been a central factor in explaining Labour's defeat at successive general elections. This revisionism was apparent from the Policy Review conducted after Labour's general election defeat in 1987. Here all main policy areas were reviewed within the context of the party. Andrew Gamble argues that one of the main results of the Policy Review was to shift policy from an isolationist tradition that emphasised the building of socialism within Britain, insulated from global constraints, to a tradition that emphasised the building of socialism within the constraints imposed by the global economy (Gamble 1992).

A changed global context is the starting point for the report's analysis. Two changes are thought to be of particular significance. First, economic changes charting 'a global revolution of finance, competition, skills and technology' (Commission on Social Justice 1994, p. 3). This adds up to an emphasis on globalisation. For the report, these changes meant there was a need to consider institutional and governance arrangements that included, but went beyond, the state. Alongside economic changes ran, secondly, profound social changes. There was in particular '*a revolution of women's life chances, of family structures and of demography*' (ibid., p. 77). Much of post-war social policy was based on an assumption of stable family units in which males were the main breadwinners in secure (typically manufacturing) employment. According to the report these assumptions had unravelled. Males no longer dominated the labour market in the ways they once had. There were now fewer manufacturing jobs, and more service and part-time work. All of this had occurred within the context of a changed family life, with the rise in divorce and of lone parenthood, and an emergence of new lifestyles outside the family. The result of such changes was that social policy had now to be recast to fit new demands and respond to new agendas.

The report *Social Justice* identified three broad responses to this changed context, labelling these the approaches of Deregulators, Levellers and Investors. Deregulators

> dream of a future in which dynamic entrepreneurs, unshackled by employment laws or social responsibilities, create new businesses and open up new markets. Theirs is a future of extremes, where the rich get richer and the poor get poorer, and where the rewards for success are matched only by the risks of failure. Economically, it depends upon the unceasing drive for competitiveness through ever-cheaper production and the pursuit of short-term profit; socially, upon the reduction of public services and public spending; politically, on a logic of centralisation, destroying institutions that stand between law-making government and individual decisions in the marketplace. (Ibid., p. 4)

For Deregulators, efficiency is the central imperative of the global economy. Individual prosperity and welfare could only be met by securing conditions for efficiency. The central mechanism for attaining efficiency was unfettered markets. In practice, this meant a limited but strong state creating conditions for a free economy. Inequality was an important part of the logic of markets for Deregulators. The prospect of high rewards helps foster appropriate incentives for entrepreneurial activity, for example. Levellers

> are pessimists, who do not see how we can turn the economy round, and in any case argue that economic renewal should not be the concern of a Commission on Social Justice. They say our job is to protect the poor from economic decay... They believe that we should try to achieve social justice primarily through the tax and benefits system. (Ibid.)

For Levellers, global changes mean markets are an inescapable feature of modernity. While Deregulators applaud, and seek to stimulate this position, Levellers focus instead on social justice, which they understand largely in terms of social exclusion, especially inequality. Rather than seeing global changes in positive terms, focus is simply made on alleviating some of its worst consequences. Levellers accept that this task is proving to be increasingly difficult. In practice, it is achieved by a reliance on tax redistribution, funded by the levelling down of the incomes of the better-off.

The third, and preferred, strategy of the report is dubbed the Investors' approach. Investors

> combine the ethics of community with the dynamics of a market economy. They believe that the extension of economic opportunity is not only the source of economic prosperity but also the basis of social justice. This demands strong social institutions, strong families and strong communities, which enable people and companies to grow, adapt and succeed. Investment in people is the top priority. (Ibid.)

For Investors, both Deregulators and Levellers largely treat issues of efficiency and social justice separately. Deregulators prioritise efficiency; Levellers social justice. However, such a separation for Investors is flawed. Against Deregulators, Investors believe that relying simply on unfettered markets does not address legitimate concerns over social justice. The central ethical value of Investors is the provision of opportunities. Given an initial unequal distribution of opportunities, unfettered markets often perpetuate or exacerbate inequalities and so do not address concerns over social exclusion. Lack of opportunity is also deemed inimical to efficiency. It leads, for example, to a suboptimal allocation of labour to jobs. Against Levellers, Investors deny exclusive focus be placed on social justice. The report states, 'we cannot have social justice without a decent measure of economic success. Social benefits have to be paid for, and the economy will not sustain limitless transfers from a diminishing section of society to an increasing class of the destitute' (ibid., pp. 18–19). Any project of social justice thus has to rely on some measure of economic success, which means a concern with efficiency. This means a positive role for markets.

To secure opportunity, core focus is placed on investment. Investment in people is identified as being the top priority. This has two strands. The first is investment in skills. The report notes, 'Lifetime learning is at the heart of our vision of a better country. By investing in skills, we can help people to realise their potential, raise their capacity to add value to the economy, take charge of their own lives and contribute to their families and communities' (ibid., p. 5). However, this emphasis on skills is combined with a focus on investment in the social infrastructure. Investors 'argue that investment in social institutions is as important as investment in economic infrastructure. At the heart of social justice is not just the idea that we owe something to each other, but the belief that we gain from giving to each other' (ibid., pp. 306–7). An important part of the investment strategies advocated centres on families, communities and local democracy. To help support families there would be an increase in child benefit (paid through income tax), reforms made to the child support system and a new statement of parental responsibilities. To help regenerate communities a National Community Regeneration Agency would be established, Community Development Trusts formed to build capacity in the local community, and small-scale credit unions set up. Proposals were advocated for housing, to allow the general release of local authorities' receipts from council housing sales, the creation of Local Housing Companies to develop and manage social rented housing, and the creation of a national Housing Bank that would help match the housing market to new family and employment conditions. To foster local democracy policies outlined decentralisation of power to Scotland and Wales (and where appropriate to the English regions), a shift of power from unelected quangos to elected bodies and greater accountability for unelected bodies. As such, an important theme has been developing investment strategies in a bottom-up context.

The focus on collectivist stakeholding is also a feature of another policy commission established to examine centre-left strategies in a contemporary context. This was the Commission on Wealth Creation and Social Cohesion set up by Paddy Ashdown, then leader of the Liberal Democrats.[2] The report set out to outline a set of principles suitable for contemporary conditions that would combine a focus on wealth creation and social cohesion, set against the background of liberal assumptions regarding a free society. Its central emphasis was the creation of a '*stakeholder* society in which companies, organisations and communities are linked to common purposes. Its members enjoy the rights and accept the obligations of *citizenship*' (Commission on Wealth Creation and Social Cohesion 1995, p. vii). As in *Social Justice*, a changed global context is the point of departure for the policy examination. In particular,

> Economic activity is increasingly internationalised. The production and diffusion of new technologies accelerates; competitive pressures intensify; both processes look set to continue for the foreseeable future. Companies and national economies ignore the challenge at their peril. This is the starting point for any analysis of the British position. (Ibid., p. iv)

Conventional wealth creation strategies are regarded by the report as increasingly ineffective in this new environment, and given that focusing on wealth was of importance for the report, owing to its contribution towards individual well-being, this pointed to different policy priorities. Whereas wealth creation had often emphasised the importance of institutional actors such as the state or firms, prime emphasis now is placed on the individual. The report states, 'The most important resources for wealth creation are human. We believe we must create a learning society, in which everyone has the opportunity to develop new skills throughout their working life' (ibid., p. ix). Skills are seen increasingly as the most important factor of production. A skilled workforce is needed in order to cope with rapid technological change. Given that technology is rapidly changing, this means a focus on lifetime learning. This priority is reinforced by the nature of global competition: to cope with increased competition Britain had to develop a comparative advantage in high quality products, implying the need for a highly skilled workforce. While compulsory education is a basic foundation for inculcating adequate skills development, particular importance is given to post-compulsory education. Rather than confining attention to a particular elite, skills acquisition has to be spread as far as possible across the population. A variety of mechanisms are suggested in this context. One of the key devices, individual learning accounts, is mentioned in the next chapter. This is because this initiative is a species of individualist rather than collectivist stakeholding. This highlights that while it is useful for analytical purposes to distinguish between collectivist and individualist accounts of stakeholding, in an important set of cases policy prescriptions combine elements of both strands. This will be one of the subjects of Chapter 5. While accepting the existence of individualist strains in this policy report, the present chapter confines its attention to moves in a collectivist direction. Wealth creation for the report had also to be considered alongside social dimensions. This pertains, specifically, to the significance placed on social cohesion. Wealth creation has to be socially sustainable, which means, for the report, a focus on social cohesion. Social cohesion 'should not be thought of as harmony, but as a condition of lively civil societies held together by a framework of citizenship' (ibid., p. 34). While social cohesion is seen as a precondition for sustainable wealth creation, the report notes that wealth-creating strategies often undid social cohesion. For example, high mobility might be conducive to wealth creation, but it is often socially disruptive. Also, income differentials may provide incentives for wealth creation, but lead to social exclusion. Indeed, a central issue for the report was how to combine wealth creation with social cohesion within the global economy.

Promoting social cohesion meant ensuring that individuals be faced with a range of opportunities. Guaranteeing opportunities meant ensuring flexibility and commitment. Flexibility allows individuals to adapt to changes wrought in the global economy. Skills here are important in supporting functional flexibility, which means individuals are capable of operating a range of tasks. But, 'what is missing in an exclusive emphasis on flexibility, is to speak of trust, of loyalty, or in our preferred phrase, of commitment' (ibid., p. 36). The report argues that a totally flexible condition is unable to generate commitment since it eschews continuity that is central to committed behaviour. To engender this, institutions have to give 'people a sense of belonging and being needed. This response by institutions is expressed by the notion that people are *stakeholders*' (ibid.). The report recognises that the roots of stakeholding lie in corporate governance. However,

> we are using the concept of stakeholders in a wider sense as well. A stakeholder society is an inclusive society. It makes every effort to involve all its citizens in the labour market, in the associations of civil society, in the political process. For citizens in turn this means that these activities, and the institutions in which they are contained, matter. They therefore engender a sense of responsibility, of obligations. (Ibid., p. 38)

This points to obligations towards others. Essentially a two-stage process is posited here. Commitment relations allow for mutual interaction over a particular period of time. Secondly, such mutual interaction helps to inculcate mutual trust. That is not to say that commitment relations are either necessary or sufficient for the emergence of such ties. On the one hand, individuals may display loyalty to one another regardless of whether they are in a long-term relationship or not. They may for instance display this by conforming to the demands of a personal morality. As such, commitment may not be necessary. Also, if mutual interaction is antagonistic, then commitment may not be sufficient for the emergence of trust. Nevertheless, for the report, commitment was an important institutional mechanism for the promotion of trust. Commitment meant that individuals were stakeholders. Reconciling wealth creation and social cohesion therefore implied a central focus on skills and responsibility.

The emphasis on flexibility and commitment implied for the report bottom-up institutions, involving a combination of markets and civil society. Markets were seen as important for fostering flexibility. More generally this pointed to the importance of competition for inculcating development. If flexibility implied a focus on markets, commitment pointed to the importance of civil society. The report noted: 'cohesive, prosperous society requires another level of intervention beyond market transactions and the bonds of individuals and their families. Networks of co-operation and reciprocity should cut across society, building trust and mutual obligation' (ibid., p. 39). Cooperation was thought to be central to civil society, and many of the proposals concern policies for promoting those non-familial institutions between state and individual. This involved, for example, 'the notion of stakeholder investors; the Private Pensions Society alongside the National Insurance Fund; Individual Learning Accounts, Community Education Trusts, a new kind of Employment Service' (ibid., p. 95). Participation in the public arena however raised a number of concerns for the report. Most importantly, 'We are aware that intermediary institutions raise difficult issues of participation and governance. Compulsory involvement is a principle that should be used sparingly in a free society. It must only be used in conjunction with effective democratic concerns' (ibid.). The report recognises that wealth creation and social cohesion might be promoted in a variety of ways. One strand, evident in countries such as Singapore, was to focus on wealth creation and social cohesion at the expense of liberty: individuals were coerced into participation in relevant arenas. Although wealth creation and social cohesion were the prime targets of the report, all strategies had to be considered against the background of liberal individualism. Conditions relating to a free society were ultimately most important. This does not mean that coercion is ruled out; in some situations it is likely to be unavoidable. Nevertheless, the presumption was that coercion ought to be minimised, and where it was thought necessary, it must always be subject to democratic control.

Public service stakeholding

Collectivist ideas have also been applied in recent times to proposals for reforming public services such as health and education. A variety of concerns have been raised about the nature of welfare services in

Britain. For example, in March 1999 the Association of Community Health Councils for England and Wales established a Commission to investigate accountability within the National Health Service (NHS).[3] One of the central conclusions of the report published in 2000 is that in 'the Commission's view the overall system of accountability is unacceptably weak. It is perhaps the least accountable of Britain's major public institutions, even though access to health is the prime concern of British citizens' (ibid., p. 8). The Commission contends that central government has been responsible for guaranteeing accountability for much of the NHS's history. It is argued that this system of accountability is too far removed from local circumstances to be fully responsive to the end-users of services. This seems to be borne out by the views of members of the public. In a poll carried out for the Commission, over two-thirds felt that services need quite a lot or a great deal of improvement.

Two broad themes are touted as ways of tackling such problems. Together they constitute 'public service stakeholding'. One notion involves an emphasis on devolution. Ed Mayo and Henrietta Moore say that this means that to a significant extent 'ownership and accountability passes from Whitehall to the direct stakeholders of public services – typically users, staff and, in some way, the broader stakeholders of the local community' (Mayo and Moore 2001, p. 21). Mayo and Moore suggest that devolution is a first step to breaking the grasp of central government. This will help create the opportunity for stakeholders to play a greater role in the running of public services. In relation to schools, for example, this creates an arena in which teachers, parents, pupils and members of the local education authority can interact more closely. For hospitals, this maps out a realm where doctors, nurses, patients and representatives from other NHS organisations can play a more active role. By hiving off institutions such as schools and hospitals (which are particular instances of what they call 'social enterprises') from the arms of central government, an opportunity is fostered for developing an area in which stakeholder interests predominate. They say that the social enterprise is 'not an arm of government: it is an independent model outside the traditions of the public sector. Typically it is led by a social entrepreneur and is socially owned or accountable. It may make profits, but they are not for private benefits. They are reinvented socially, either in service or in the community' (ibid., p. 26). This allows for the 'emergence of "horizontal accountability", in which the immediate stakeholders – the local people and organizations who are in the best position to judge what is going on – hold public service organizations to account' (ibid., p. 29). This stance is seen in a key proposal of the Commission on the NHS. The Commission states that their 'central proposal for reform of the NHS is that the service should be made more open and accountable through a constitution of its own' (ibid., p. 72). The constitution would protect the principles underpinning the NHS and establish it at arm's length from the government. A charter for patients detailing how they should be properly treated (for instance in relation to waiting times) would be a core part of the constitution.

Alongside devolution there is secondly a focus on participation. A number of themes inform strategies for participation. One strand involves the provision of information – it is often felt that individuals need access to appropriate information if they are to get the best out of participation. There is a focus, accordingly, on ensuring that they have access to adequate information. The Commission on the NHS, for instance, recommends that the public should be given access to the minutes of all meetings as well as the policy papers of all executive and advisory boards within the NHS (subject to constraints regarding individual privacy). Attention is also paid to opening up spaces in which individuals can actively engage. This takes a variety of forms, overlapping with the sorts of proposal advocated within the context of corporate governance. For example, one way of securing the participation of patients in the running of hospitals is to allow for the representation of patients on hospital boards. Alternatively, separate patient bodies could be established which hospital managers have to consult when fashioning and implementing a policy.

Conclusion

Knowledge and responsibility

Having looked at the different dimensions of corporate governance stakeholding and public service stakeholding, this chapter now considers the important ideas that inform the way collectivist stakeholding developed in Britain. Two themes dominate collectivist models of stakeholding, namely a focus on responsibility and on knowledge. The stress on responsibility is seen, for example, on the importance individuals such as John Kay attach to fostering cooperation and trust within firms. It is also seen in the role mutual obligations play in models focusing on mutual education. With respect to knowledge, collectivist strands stress how knowledge is created internal to a social practice. This is seen, for example, in Kay's model of organisational knowledge. Mutual education implies similarly that individuals learn through interaction with others. Responsibility and knowledge are deliberately combined. This is because of the importance attached to the relationship between them. This stresses, first, the importance of cooperation for skill formation. The creation of knowledge in a social context in particular often requires some prior sharing of information. In relation to mutual education, for instance, in order to grow individuals must first share information amongst each other. If cooperation is thought to support skill formation, certain skills are also thought important for responsibilities towards others. To cooperate in the exchange of information, individuals need to be skilled at identifying and preparing appropriate information. Collective models of stakeholding generally display both instrumental and intrinsic values, although the mix of these values varies across different accounts. Instrumental value means stakeholding is a useful mechanism for achieving a particular objective. The instrumental dimensions to these models can be seen, for example, within the context of corporate governance. The perceived contribution to profits has often been seen as one of the key strengths of stakeholding (Plender 1997). But profits also have intrinsic value: that is, stakeholding is also an end in itself. Fostering cooperation can be seen as being valuable in its own right, possessing independent value.

One issue of importance is whether the distinction between responsibility and knowledge can always be sustained. Skills are often individualist in orientation. This is seen, for example, in those accounts of knowledge that emphasise the role of 'natural talents'. These constitute an important set of models of knowledge acquisition. Natural talents refer to the innate capacity for learning which is located within each individual, with different people possessing different innate capacities (so talents differ between individuals). Any acquisition of knowledge based on natural talents is, accordingly, individualist in orientation. Social capital points however to ties between persons, with the result that many types of knowledge fall outside a social capital remit. Conversely, certain types of social capital, such as trust, are unlikely to be viewed as a type of skill. As such, important parts of social capital fall outside a knowledge arena. Responsibility and knowledge can, on the above instances, be clearly separated. This is not to say that there are no areas of overlap. 'Social skills' (such as communication and presentational skills) are an arena where human and social capital overlap. Although knowledge and responsibility are not mutually exclusive, there are realms where they do not intersect. As such, a distinction between knowledge and responsibility ought to be maintained.

Tensions

The above does not imply that the emphasis on responsibility and knowledge is free from tensions or problems. On the one hand tensions exist within both responsibility and knowledge. With regard to knowledge, a tension exists between specific and general skills. Much of this focus of knowledge within collective models concentrates on knowledge internal and specific to a particular practice. However, social capital is also intended to help foster the acquisition of other skills, which include general skills. Whereas specific skills tie individuals to a particular workplace, general skills facilitate movement elsewhere. Although an individual's skills portfolio is likely to involve an important role for both (combining general computer literacy skills, for example, with knowledge of particular production procedures), at important junctures there is likely to be tension between these skills and an individual will face a trade-off between acquiring further specific or general skills. With regard to responsibility, gains engendered by fostering cooperation may be offset by losses from going beyond personal responsibility. Trying to accommodate others may impose a series of costs (when individuals fail to coordinate, for example, despite the best of intentions) that may be avoided when individuals simply take responsibility for their own interests. On the other hand, tensions exist between knowledge and responsibility. An established set of bonds between individuals may hinder innovation when individuals are not encouraged to break with set practices and try new ideas. Although these (and other) considerations indicate that the focus on responsibility and knowledge is not unproblematic, they do not imply that the difficulties are likely to be insurmountable. There are important spaces in which (as noted above) they can, plausibly, be profitably combined. This facilitates the emergence of important stakeholder notions.

Summary

This chapter has examined collectivist accounts of stakeholding. The purpose of this is to establish whether a coherent set of principles can be detected within this strand of stakeholding. The chapter has focused on the strongest theoretical accounts within this context. It has been suggested that at the heart of the corporate governance and public service agendas that constitute the collectivist approach is a view that emphasises promoting responsibility and knowledge organised around the possession of stakes. It is true that this involves some measure of simplification. Important differences exist between different theorists. A trade-off is faced when fixing the mix between common themes and differences. It is suggested, nevertheless, that these differences are best analysed within a common framework of fostering responsibility and knowledge organised around the possession of stakes. Differences exist mainly over the nature of responsibility and knowledge, as well as within the institutional context appropriate for fostering this. Having covered the first of the two main strands of stakeholding, the next chapter is devoted to looking at the other main component of individualist stakeholding.

3
Individualist Stakeholding

The issue of how resources should be shared across society is one of the most important and long-standing questions in politics and economics. Individuals usually depend on resources in order to help fulfil their goals and ambitions. The stock of resources in any society is, however, finite. The potentially infinite set of ways in which resources can be deployed means that the existing stock of resources is unlikely to fully service the aims and aspirations of all individuals across society. This problem of scarcity means that the question of how resources should be distributed across society is a significant one. Two themes have attracted particular attention in discussions about the proper distribution of resources. First, the idea that all people should be treated equally exerts important influence. It asserts that no individual should be deprived of access to resources through unfortunate circumstances. It is not fair, for example, for a person to suffer a lack of resources simply because they were unlucky enough to be born into a poor family. A second theme draws attention to the importance of rewarding effort. This defends the view that individuals have legitimate claims over resources which they have expended effort in order to accumulate. If individuals invest resources in order to acquire further resources, rather than simply consuming existing resources, then they are entitled to have a share of the fruits of their endeavour.

These standpoints are not always easy to reconcile. Allowing individuals to have a claim over any investments they make, for instance, means endorsing that these people should enjoy a greater share of resources than others who, facing a similar set of circumstances, choose to invest rather than consume. Rewarding effort here permits the existence of inequality. There is, nevertheless, a long-standing tradition in politics that has sought to combine both concerns. It can be traced back at least to Thomas Paine. Like many accounts in this tradition, Paine's model starts from an idealised state to create a benchmark with which the actually existing distribution of property may be judged. He draws special attention to the distribution of material resources. He supported the idea that social justice requires that all individuals be paid a capital grant. In *Agrarian Justice* Paine argued that everything originally was common property (Paine 1987). He argued that at any subsequent point no individual should be worse off than they would have been under this original state. While private appropriation and cultivation of land had led to benefits for many, it had left many others worse off than they would have been under the original state. Since only value added to the land for Paine could be claimed as private property, Paine argued for the right for all individuals deprived of their natural inheritance to be compensated for their loss. A 10 per cent tax on the capital value of property would enable all those reaching age 21 to receive £15 and all those over 50 to receive £10 (Macfarlane 1996). Modern exponents of this tradition include individuals such as Ronald Dworkin. One of the features of Dworkin's account is that he considers non-material as well as material resources. He argues that showing individuals equal concern is the most important or sovereign value in social justice. Showing individuals equal concern means ensuring that any inequalities that arise between people have their roots in choice not bad brute luck. Brute luck covers situations to which individuals have not voluntarily subjected themselves; it is usually contrasted with 'option luck', namely those gambles which individuals have voluntarily accepted. An important part of brute luck encompasses individual resources. These resources refer to material endowments and natural talents. This does not mean that Dworkin regards all inequalities as being unfair; those rooted in choice are generally seen as fair. For example, he regards inequalities that arise between an individual who chooses to engage in work rather than leisure as compared to an identically placed individual who chooses to engage in leisure rather than work as fair. This is not to say that brute luck and choice can always be neatly separated. Individuals' choice to invest in skills may be affected by their natural talent. The greater the natural talent, the greater the likelihood that individuals will choose to develop their talent. However, although brute luck may play a role in determining choice, choice will also be affected by factors independent of brute luck. Two identically placed individuals can nevertheless choose to invest different amounts in developing their knowledge. Although brute luck and choice may overlap, they can nevertheless be separated (Dworkin 2000).

Dworkin's logic points to the importance of trying to ensure that any inequalities that arise have their roots in choice not luck. The left has often relied on using the taxation system to redistribute resources once inequalities have already arisen. But, as Stuart White points out, this is likely to be a blunt tool for separating out choice and luck inequalities (since it is difficult to distinguish between choice and luck components in resultant inequality). A better-targeted policy may be to focus on ensuring that individuals have equal endowments of resources. Although White does not deny the importance of redistributive taxation as part of an overall package of centre-left policies directed at tackling inequality, this emphasis on endowments may help ensure that any inequalities that emerge are due to choice, not bad brute luck (White 1997). These debates are noteworthy because they provided an important impetus behind discussions of 'individualist stakeholding' that arose in Britain during the 1990s. This tradition of stakeholding advocates providing individuals with their own stakes or assets. This chapter considers how this individualist strand is constructed in Britain. It does this by contemplating the areas of the economy and welfare in which individualist accounts emerged, and then articulating the common assumptions that underpin these discussions. It is shown that individualist accounts focus on promoting individual responsibility and skills organised around the possession of stakes.

Individualist stakeholding

In Britain individualist stakeholding emerged within two main spheres, namely an economic and a welfare domain. Within the economic arena individualist stakeholding ideas surfaced to an important extent in reaction to the application of collectivist stakeholding to corporate governance. David Soskice expresses many of the criticisms of corporate governance stakeholding from this perspective (see Leadbeater and Mulgan 1996a; 1996b for a similar argument). For David Soskice, much of the basis of corporate governance stakeholding drew essentially upon an analysis of German capitalism. Here attention was drawn to the supposed efficiency benefits and moral purchase of cooperation achieved through long-termism. He argued however that with regard to Britain such capitalism was neither feasible nor desirable. The feasibility argument rested on the view that it was not possible to develop the institutional context that supports German cooperative capitalism in Britain (Soskice has expanded on some of these themes in Soskice (1999)). In particular German capitalism was supported by a set of interlocking institutions, and was itself a product of its particular historical and cultural development. To replicate this, according to Soskice, would imply far-reaching, and ultimately infeasible, changes in the nature of British capitalism. Like Hutton, this analyses capitalism largely as a system. Soskice's understanding of stakeholding rests thus in part upon assumptions regarding institutional possibilities within the British economy. Soskice's analysis of Germany's 'company level training system' helps illustrate some themes here. This company level training model meant companies offered a system of apprenticeships that contributed to Germany's good record on intermediate training, a source of its industrial strength and a key example of its cooperative capitalism. Soskice argues that this company level training system rested upon a particular network of interlocking institutions. For school-leavers not destined for higher or further education, incentives to engage in such company level training would be enhanced (if they were to exist at all) by the prospect of stable employment with adequate returns after training. Such an employment contract would typically be provided by the training firm. But in order for a firm to provide such a contract, a number of conditions need to be met. First, there is a need to ensure that other employers do not engage in the poaching of staff, otherwise free-riding will reduce, and possibly halt, the supply of such contracts. Employer coordination is achieved in Germany principally through employers' associations. Secondly, employers also need to recoup the costs of training. This would be achieved by paying individuals at a rate below their marginal product of labour for a limited post-training time period. Such a wage would be sustained if individuals did not attempt to renegotiate this wage post-training. This was to be secured through unions, where unions promised to ensure that individuals did not attempt to renegotiate contracts. A third element involved financial institutions. In order to secure steady demand for labour, employers needed to be assured that financial institutions would not place instant pressure on labour-shedding during slack periods in the economy. But financial institutions needed to be assured in turn that resources were being used efficiently. In practice this was achieved by having representation of financial institutions on company boards. The apparently simple system of company level training depended therefore on a much wider set of supportive institutions. These complexities multiplied when going beyond the company level system to embrace other aspects of cooperative capitalism. For Soskice, it is not feasible to develop institutions characteristic of Germany in the UK.

Even if we reject this, Soskice argues that it is not desirable in any case to try to replicate German capitalism. Soskice contends that British capitalism has compensating advantages, indeed given its persistence it would be strange if this were not the case. The short-term relationships that tend to dominate British capitalism are a source for Soskice of a variety of advantages. One strand to this relates to innovation. Soskice believes that this is better enhanced by short-term rather than long-term relations: short-term relations are more conducive towards innovation and the discovery of knowledge by permitting individuals to embark on a wide variety of experimental relationships and engaging frequently in trial and error. Another area that Soskice highlights concerns financial services. Such sectors, he argues, are characterised by short-term relationships, and British capitalism displays a comparative advantage in the provision of such services. Soskice argues further that these areas are likely to increase in importance within the global economy. An implication of this is that British capitalism might in fact now be better suited to meet future challenges. But Soskice combines this with a moral critique of German capitalism. He argues in particular that certain individuals are unfairly excluded from long-term relationships in German capitalism. He cites in particular the case of women, arguing that in countries like Germany employers are discouraged from employing females owing to the expectation that the female labour supply is likely to be interrupted by periodic labour market withdrawal arising from pregnancy and their traditional role in bearing most of the responsibility of child-rearing. As a result, such employers do not give opportunities to women, and in fact discriminate against them. In an economy dominated by short-term relationships, this source of discrimination is largely absent. Soskice argues that this may be detected in the career prospects of women in the UK and Germany: females have better opportunities for both work and progression in Britain than in Germany (Soskice 1997).

Labour market stakeholding

For Soskice however, this does not mean that the idea of stakeholding ought to be dispensed with entirely. Instead he advocates 'labour market' stakeholding. This can 'cut with the grain of liberal market economies and help us think in more innovative ways' (Soskice 1997, p. 224). He argues,

> Stakeholding is an implicit contract between the state and the individual citizen. The fact that it is a contract means that both sides have obligations and receive benefits ... benefits only accrue to those who have carried out the relevant obligations. Also, the citizen has a choice about how much to 'invest' in the contract. Some may invest more than others. (Ibid., p. 223)

Soskice aims to substitute an emphasis upon rights and obligations or responsibilities for the conventional liberal discourse of a universal entitlement to rights. This is a general characterisation that extends beyond the realm of economics. Soskice has paid particular attention however to developing this in an economic context. Here, this general characterisation manifests itself primarily through labour market stakeholding. This has two main elements. First, 'an implicit contract that serious investment effort by a young person at school should lead to the acquisition of the relevant general and social skills necessary for the modern labour market' (ibid., p. 224). Soskice sees skills as being a particularly important determinant of collective efficiency and individual opportunity and security in the future. While skills issues are important across the board, particular attention has been paid by Soskice to the participation rate in intermediate vocational education and training which he argues is a particular failure in Britain. Any credible policy must tackle this area. One step is to insist that individuals must be serious about their own training needs. A core problem here, however, is that individuals have little incentive to engage in such training, given that they face poor opportunities after training. As such, the focus should be on providing appropriate opportunities. While subsidies to low-level employment in the private sector may offer employment opportunities, they do not typically offer ladders for career progression. To tackle this, government should consider low-level public sector careers providing such opportunities. Soskice emphasises therefore obligations on both sides of this contract. The second element is individual learning accounts (ILA). Within an ILA each individual would possess a learning account dedicated to providing funds for their training needs. Individuals would provide capital within this account, with matching contributions by firms and government. The account would provide a source of capital for a set of approved courses. Such an account, 'puts the emphasis on the individual – through the individual's obligations to invest in his or her own training in order to attract corresponding subsidies by employer and state, and through the individual's choice in how *much* to invest and where to train' (ibid., p. 225). Although various efficiency justifications may be given to support ILAs, Soskice focuses on personal responsibility. One important theme stressed here is the setting up of incentives to help inculcate the appropriate sense of personal responsibility. This is usually achieved by emphasising individual ownership stakes. Allowing individuals to keep a substantial part of any surplus generated through individual ownership, such as individual learning accounts, gives them an incentive to develop the appropriate sense of personal responsibility. That is not to say that incentives are either necessary or sufficient for the inculcation of personal responsibility. The fact that individual responsibility need not necessarily coincide with a person's self-interest means that responsibility is unlikely to be inculcated by incentives alone. Nevertheless insofar as rational self-interest is an important part of human motivations for theorists of stakeholding means that incentives cannot be ignored, even if ultimately institutions go beyond their provision.

Individual learning accounts were also advocated by the Commission on Wealth Creation and Social Cohesion. Their report notes, 'Such a system recognises the need for employees to develop their skills continually in order to build their careers, and also recognises that while employers cannot offer lifetime employment, they have a responsibility to promote lifetime employability' (Commission on Wealth Creation and Social Cohesion 1995, p. 80).

Given that employers enjoyed the benefits from having trained workers, they also had a reciprocal obligation towards employees. The report recognises that this cannot be through the provision of lifelong employment, and argues instead that the focus ought to be on helping secure lifetime employability. Since employability depends largely on skills, this means that employers have to be involved in skills acquisition, in particular through funding arrangements. These arguments are applied more generally to the other entities involved in ILAs. The government has an obligation to help fund these accounts since it also benefits from a skilled workforce, for example through tax revenues. Given that individuals most obviously benefit from skills, in terms of trapping the benefits of training, they also face a responsibility to invest in their own training. This underlines the point that skills are tied to responsibility.

Popular capitalism

Individualist accounts of stakeholding also draw on debates in a welfare context. These ideas can be traced in recent times to popular capitalism. Emerging during the Thatcher administrations, popular capitalism focused on spreading individual ownership as widely as possible across the population. This was *popular* since this emphasised spreading ownership as far as possible across the population, and *capitalism* since the particular ownership form stressed was private property. Popular capitalism was part of the attempt by Conservatives to roll back the frontiers of the state whose intervention was thought to imply important inefficiencies. With regard to society, one important set of issues related to concerns over a dependency culture. Individual ownership was one of the mechanisms used to try to foster personal responsibility. Ivor Crewe noted,

> The Thatcher administration was far more determined than previous Conservative governments had been to reshape the social structure. The government's first priority was to spread individual property ownership more widely than before, in the name of individual "self-sufficiency" and "responsibility".
>
> (Crewe 1993, p. 15)

By allowing individuals to appropriate gains through personal ownership, this was thought to provide incentives to be self-reliant.

Although a variety of different ownership forms could have been the subject of attention, particular emphasis was placed on home-ownership. Part of the reason for this related to the fact that home-ownership has been a salient theme of post-war Conservatism. Important during policy discussions in the 1940s and 1950s, ownership of a house was seen as a basic human instinct (Ramsden 1980). Moreover home-ownership was thought to be a significant means through which individuals could properly develop their personality. This was set out, for example, in a speech Anthony Eden made to the Conservative Party Conference on 3 October 1946 (Baker 1993). Housing also attracted attention since it was viewed as an important example of state involvement, through council houses. The sale of council houses, accordingly, would help roll back the frontiers of this state intervention.

Popular capitalism was also used as a device to reduce the scope of state activity in the economy. As seen in Chapter 1, owing to arguments from individuals such as Hayek as well as public choice theorists, Conservatives believed that public officials lacked the information or incentives to make efficient economic decisions. Conservatives believed that efficiency would be improved if the state withdrew from the economy. In policy terms, one theme that attracted Conservative interest was the sale of state assets through privatisation. During the 1980s share flotations were offered in prominent nationalised industries and services such as the railways, British Gas and British Telecommunications. Popular capitalism was integral to this. John Redwood notes,

> part of the vitality of the free enterprise system comes from allowing people to generate ideas, and from giving them their heads so that they can prosper. In the West the link is being forged through the process of popular capitalist sales of assets from the state to private individuals.
>
> (Redwood 1988, p. 155)

It was thought that personal ownership would enhance efficiency by providing incentives to be entrepreneurial (through risk-taking, innovation and the competitive search for profitable opportunities). For Thatcherites maximising incentives meant strengthening the claims of individuals over any surplus generated from property. This meant a project of emphasising rights over property. One of the important ways in which this was manifested was in debates over taxation. Conservatives were committed, at least in principle, to reducing the burden of taxation on property. Markets were taken to support entrepreneurial activity because they were thought to constitute the best discovery mechanism allowing efficient trial-and-error, as well as helping to foster competition which provided a spur to innovation. The dependency critique pointed in similar directions. In particular, this suggested the importance of bottom-up institutions. Although, in general, such institutions cover both civil society and markets, the Conservatives placed emphasis on markets for the development of responsibility.

Popular capitalism was associated with a widening of individual ownership. Ivor Crewe noted, for example, that the percentage of shareholders in the population increased from 7 per cent in 1979 to 25 per cent in 1991. Home ownership rose from 52 per cent in 1979 to 66 per cent in 1989 (Crewe 1993). By the mid-1990s, however, the attempts to foster popular capitalism had been scaled down. A variety of explanations for this may be offered. One important set of reasons plausibly relates to the way in which popular capitalism was constructed. Difficulties in the central instrument used by Conservatives to counter dependency in society probably contributed to the scaling down of Conservative ambitions. In general, focusing resources in a limited amount of assets could make individuals prone to high levels of risk if such assets were volatile. Although opportunities exist for diversifying risk for share-ownership, this is difficult to foster for home-ownership. This became a problem when changes in interest rate policy wrought by altered macroeconomic circumstances meant an increase in mortgage payments. Some of those who had borrowed could no longer afford these, leading to 'negative equity'. Proposals to extend home-ownership were probably not appealing to Conservatives in such a situation. Similarly, the sale of state economic assets provided the main context for spreading share-ownership within popular capitalism. By the mid-1990s the privatisation of such state assets was curtailed. Many of the obvious candidates for privatisation had already been sold off, and public support seemed less widespread for further privatisations. Public ambivalence over privatisation did not mean that the support for individual ownership was necessarily dimmed, since this could have been developed in other spheres. But, since Conservatives were not inclined to intervene in the affairs of private corporations to help secure a wider distribution of ownership, the curtailment of the privatisation programme fed into the curtailment of the project of spreading share-ownership.

Stakeholder welfare

Popular capitalism was important for the centre-left. Interest in stakeholding was an early manifestation of the attempt to construct a left popular capitalism. Gavin Kelly, when reviewing John Plender's *A Stake in the Future: the Stakeholder Solution*, argued, '*Stake in the Future* makes a significant contribution to the spate of books seeking to flesh out the stakeholder theme ... If the centre left is to invent its own notion of popular capitalism this would be a good place to start' (Kelly 1997, p. 163). Commentating on popular capitalism Bruce Ackerman and Anne Alstott note that Margaret Thatcher 'created a new property-owning citizenry, and she won vast popularity in the process' (Ackerman and Alstott 1998, p. 12). They mention this to highlight the potential support for their own advocacy of stakeholding in the United States. Charles Leadbeater and Geoff Mulgan argue similarly that stakeholding is 'an idea with huge potential for popular appeal. People are attracted by the idea that they should have a tangible stake in the company they work for. Baroness Thatcher tapped into this with her vision – still unrealised – of popular capitalism and a share-owning democracy' (Leadbeater and Mulgan 1996a). The importance of popular capitalism for the centre-left emanated from a variety of sources. Part of this reflected feasibility considerations. For many reformists, popular capitalism altered the context in which any reformist project was to emerge in important ways. Centre-left strategies had to emerge, for example, in a context in which individual shareholders now exceeded trade unionists. Many conventional appeals and strategies had to be recast to fit this changed context. However, a project organised around popular capitalism was also attractive for the centre-left in its own right. Altering the distribution of ownership resonated with traditional reformist concerns. Moreover such a policy was likely to be popular. There seemed to be widespread support for a policy of distributing ownership.

Welfare was an important site for the emergence of these models. Frank Field provided an important account within a British context.

As well as making a number of theoretical contributions (Field 2000; 1996a; 1996b), his work was important at a policy level through his role as a minister at the Department for Social Security charged with examining welfare reform, as well as through his participation in the Commission on Wealth Creation and Social Cohesion examined below. Although Field's spell as minister was shortlived, the reference to stakeholder pensions that survived his time in office is in significant part a legacy of his involvement. Field's account is set against selective or targeted welfare. For Field this was problematic since it helped to foster, rather than undermine, a dependency culture. The feature singled out for most criticism is the means test. He argues, 'Means tests are the cancer within the welfare state, rotting decent values and overwhelming the honesty and dignity of recipients in almost equal proportions' (Field 1996b, p. 9). Field argues first that means tests penalise those individuals who seek to go beyond any minimally defined benefit standard by the partial or complete withdrawal of benefit. This sets up poor incentives because individuals have little reason to go beyond such standards. But secondly this has adverse character consequences in terms of fostering a dependency culture. Individuals become locked into a culture in which, rather than depend upon themselves, they come to depend solely on the state. This helps erode their personal character. He argues, 'means tests are the most potent recruiting sergeant there is for the dependency culture' (ibid., p. 17). Tackling this, for Field, meant reaffirming a commitment to universal welfare at the heart of conventional social democratic welfare policy. Universalism would lay a floor above which individuals could make additional welfare provision and not be penalised for the exercise of good character. Although he supports this universal commitment, Field departs from conventional social democratic welfare policy in at least two important ways. First, for him it relied too heavily on altruistic sentiments. Policy should instead be reconstructed to give a greater role for self-interest. Field felt this was a lesson learnt from Thatcherites. He argues, 'No welfare system can function effectively if it is not based on a realistic view of human nature. Self-interest, not altruism, is mankind's main driving force' (ibid., p. 19). This does not mean however that altruism plays no role in Field's account. Indeed, he insists that notions of altruism are embedded within his account from the inception, only that this will emerge once stakeholder arrangements driven by self-interest are shown to work. For Field the lack of attention paid to self-interest within conventional social democracy helps explain the problems it encountered. Universalism within conventional social democracy was sustained by redistribution from the better to the less well off. As welfare burdens rose, this transfer of resources became politically more difficult to sustain. Although redistribution remained important for Field, tackling it meant concentrating more closely on how welfare policy also appealed to self-interest. He argues that a key implication of this general task is that 'any new settlement will be dominated by the emerging values which prize ownership and control' (ibid., p. 11). He argues that individual ownership may help promote the development of responsibility consonant with the emphasis given to self-interest. Individuals would be rewarded for the exercise of good character because they would recoup benefits of this via ownership of welfare capital. This makes a connection between personal contributions and benefits. It also points to welfare in which the right to draw from insurance when in periods of difficulty is matched by a corresponding responsibility to contribute when in work. This implies a welfarism that is continually active, in contrast to the assumptions of the post-war welfare state when the welfare state was active when individuals were passive, and passive when individuals were active. A second important departure relates the conventional social democratic emphasis on the state for funding and provision of welfare. For Field this downplayed the constraints facing efficient state intervention, and the role the state could still play in fostering dependence. Instead more attention should be paid to fostering provision through civil society.

Stakeholder pensions

'Stakeholder pensions' provide an important example of Field's approach. He contended that a focus on pensions was of core importance, as pension expenditure constituted the largest single item on social security expenditure, itself the largest single item of government expenditure. Furthermore, a variety of changes made reform in this area of central importance. Demographic changes such as the general ageing of the population meant the future of pensions was a pressing concern. There were, in addition, changes in employment conditions which meant that the previous pension settlement that rested largely upon an assumption of stable male employment was increasingly untenable. Field argued that pensions provided fertile ground for the development of stakeholder ideas for a number of reasons. First, there appeared to be a constituency supportive of change. Pension reform through the 1980s, with the encouragement of private pension provision, had proved to be popular. Demand for personal private pensions, Field argued, was unabated, even after accounting for various scandals such as mis-selling. The general support for change could therefore be directed to promote a stakeholder agenda. Second, this might be an attractive area for stakeholders since it involved the distribution and nature of ownership rights. Field's stakeholder pension scheme is a compulsory privately funded second pension scheme. This builds upon the basic state pension, which would be used to help secure an income that would be guaranteed to all pensioners. The basic state pension is a pay-as-you-go scheme based upon an inter-generational contract, that is, each generation in the labour force funds the pension of the preceding (and now retired) generation through the taxation system. Although this relies on the state, its complete reform is likely to be difficult. Its abolition would imply that the final generation would have to honour existing pledges as well as make provisions for their own pension provision that would be difficult, politically, to implement. As time progresses however, the shift towards funded provision will allow state provision to retract. In a funded system, each person pays contributions to a personal fund which is invested in the stock market, and from which pension benefits are drawn once retired. Funded pensions, for Field, would strengthen the link between a person's pension contribution and the benefits they receive. Funded pensions, however, in contrast to a pay-as-you-go system, focus on defining contributions rather than benefits. The success of funded pensions depends on the performance of investments made in the stock market. Where returns are poor, simply relying on funded pensions may be insufficient to provide adequate security in retirement. Securing a minimum income guarantee may, here, have resort to conventional state redistribution. This means that utilising pay-as-you-go elements alongside a shift towards funded pensions may reflect desirability as well as feasibility concerns.

Asset-based welfare

This approach to welfare was acted upon in other countries with a focus on asset-based welfare. Many ideas discussed in a British context were influenced by academic writing in the United States. Michael Sherraden's account of stakeholding was important, for example, for various policy measures that were discussed within the IPPR, where he was invited to speak in 2000 about his ideas. For Sherraden a common theme across both right and left was the view that tackling poverty implied a central focus on income redistribution after inequalities have arisen (Sherraden 1991, 1990). Although left and right disagree over the merits of such an approach, for Sherraden both nonetheless agree that proper debates over welfare should be conducted within these boundaries. He argues for an alternative perspective concentrating on initial holdings of wealth, because they are likely to be more important for strategies to escape poverty. For Sherraden this approach allows individuals both to realise opportunities which would remain formal without access to resources, and to focus on strategies for escaping poverty rather than ameliorating the worst consequences of failing to realise opportunities. He argues that inequalities are more marked as to initial holdings of wealth, rather than income, and that focusing on initial holdings rather than redistribution is a better-targeted policy since it concentrates on a root cause, rather than on the symptoms, of poverty. The focus on initial endowments is not confined simply to wealth however, and covers a range of different assets. For example, attention has also been given to ownership of Individual Development Accounts that contain resources to help fund individual development such as skill acquisition (Sherraden, Page-Adams and Johnson 1999). As such, this is generally referred to as asset-based welfare.

Capital grants

Another set of proposals important for British theorists is the provision of universal capital grants. In the context of the United States, Ackerman and Alstott suggest that capital grants worth $80,000 be paid to all individuals once they graduate from high school. Individuals would be able to use these grants as they please, although Ackerman and Alstott expect they will be used for investment purposes to help fund a variety of life projects. Resources for the grant would be raised initially by a communal tax. This reflects the 'community's obligation to give each person equal respect by providing her with equal resources to develop her unique talents' (Ackerman and Alstott 1998, p. 193). After the first grants had been paid, a fund would be established to which grant-recipients would contribute at the end of their lives. In this way, the scheme would eventually become self-financing. Ackerman and Alstott distinguish their policy from proposals in favour of basic income. In contrast to the one-off capital grant proposals, advocates of a basic income suggest making a stream of payments at regular intervals, typically annually. Although the eventual amount received by individuals under either scheme may be the same (if the total value of the stream of basic income payments adds up to the capital grant payment), grants allow individuals to have instant access to the whole income (although this may be partially affected by the extent to which individuals can use their basic income as collateral for borrowing on capital markets). According to Ackerman and Alstott, instant access to the whole capital expands the range of investment opportunities available for individuals. They contend that this allows individuals to make a more meaningful difference to their personal position than any opportunities afforded by a basic income. In a British context Gavin Kelly and Rachel Lissauer have advocated a system of capital grants to be given to all individuals when they reach eighteen. The capital grants would then be used to help individuals realise any life plans (Kelly and Lissauer 2000; Kelly 2000). For the Fabian Society Julian Le Grand and David Nissan have argued for conditional capital grants, whereby individuals would only be able to use any grants for prescribed purposes. They suggest that a supervisory board, comprising for example a person's guardians and a fund-manager, would oversee any money spent. Money would be earmarked for certain purposes, such as skills investments, and the supervisory board would only release money after approving appropriate spending plans (Le Grand and Nissan 1999; Le Grand and Nissan 2000).

Differences between left and right

The above centre-left accounts can be distinguished from popular capitalism in several important respects. First, centre-left accounts place greater emphasis on collective mechanisms for instituting stakeholding. Thatcherites tended to rely primarily on the market in the construction of their version of stakeholding. Although the market is important for centre-left accounts, greater emphasis is placed on civil society as a supplement to, or a way of helping control, markets. Although the emphasis on shares in companies within popular capitalism illustrates that collective institutions played some role in Thatcherite accounts, centre-left approaches go beyond corporations to focus more generally on institutions in civil society. Some theorists suggest in fact that the lack of emphasis on collective institutions in Thatcherism may be seen in the treatment of the corporation. For Colin Crouch and David Marquand, the corporation in free market thought was treated as if it were simply an individual, rather than recognising that it is a collective institution made up of differing components (Crouch and Marquand 1995). The refusal to see the corporation as a collective institution for Crouch and Marquand resulted from the importance of a free-market individualistic ideology. Secondly, greater emphasis is placed on the responsibilities as well as rights of property in centre-left accounts. This springs in large part from greater emphasis on cooperation in centre-left accounts. Thirdly, there is more emphasis on equality in centre-left accounts. Andrew Gamble and Gavin Kelly argue that popular capitalism did not adequately tackle the uneven distribution of ownership. A left agenda would imply a more concerted attempt to spread individual ownership (Gamble and Kelly 1996a). Some of the differences between left and right accounts can be seen by considering conservative criticisms of centre-left proposals. Robert Skidelsky has criticised Ackerman's and Alstott's proposals from a conservative perspective. These criticisms are rooted partly in technical concerns; they are off-target, because at 21, Skidelsky argues, for those who have been through college the grants are not needed, since they have already financed their studies from other sources. For others, this grant comes too late to give them an incentive to invest in a college education. This argument tends, however, to support a policy of paying the grant earlier rather than, as Skidelsky puts forward, not paying it at all. Notwithstanding this, this objection considers skills acquisition simply in terms of acquisition of a college education. Seen in terms of a project of lifelong learning, however, means that individuals could still use the grant to fund future investment in skills. Moreover, in Ackerman's and Alstott's case, the grant could be used to finance a range of projects in addition to skills.

A second technical objection relates to administrative problems that Skidelsky associates with the scheme. Rather than reducing an already over-extended state, this proposal, for Skidelsky, will add extra layers of bureaucracy and lead to complications in tax collection. Although it is true that the scheme that Ackerman and Alstott advocate will point initially to the importance of a new tax, it is likely that the tax implications will be simplified once the scheme becomes self-financing. Furthermore the scheme is relatively simple to administer. Once operational, it may be possible to streamline other forms of welfare provision, permitting possible reductions in state intervention elsewhere. As such, the administrative problems that Skidelsky raises may not be as severe as he suggests. More substantive conservative concerns are revealed in his critique of redistribution. For Skidelsky the provision of universal capital grants represents a redistributive agenda, and the fact that such an agenda is thought important ignores the fact that 'the market system itself is an equalizing force of unique power' (Skidelsky 2000, p. 8). However, even if non-market intervention were needed to secure redistribution, this would be unjustified since it would imply 'continuous redistributions to offset inequalities of earning power arising from an unequal distribution of talents. This is incompatible with natural justice, private property, liberty and much else which makes a free society possible' (ibid.).

Redistribution need not, however, be incompatible with natural justice, private property and liberty. A coherent justification can be given, for example, in terms of correcting brute luck inequalities. Rather than demonstrating that left models of redistribution are unprincipled Skidelsky's criticisms highlight different attitudes towards equality between left and right. A different objection that he raises contends that capital grants undermine the importance of communal ties. In particular, the proposal is anti-family since it ignores the importance of family ties in favour of individual interests and, since families are the basis of communities, this undermines communal ties. It is not clear however that these proposals are either anti-family or anti-community. These proposals may help address some concerns raised about families. Feminists charge, for example, that family life in fact disguises inequalities of power because men unjustly exploit and dominate females. Capital grants, by providing an independent source of income for all members of a family, have the potential to reduce such inequalities. This could in fact help to bolster family life at a time in which there is greater awareness and reaction against these traditional inequalities. Capital grants are also couched in terms of duty towards others (with obligations to fund capital grants for future generations for example).

Rather than showing these grants are anti-family and anti-community, Skidelsky does highlight that the nature of intervention is likely to differ between left and right accounts.

General model

Individualist accounts place greater emphasis on individuals being authors of their own lives. This attention reflects a concern with autonomy that makes individual choice central. Some indication that individual choice is important for such accounts is given by a general emphasis on self-interest. Frank Field, for example, argues that self-interest should be the starting point for constructing any model of stakeholding since this is the most powerful human instinct. The focus on self-interest often leads to an examination of incentives in such accounts. Choice supposes the existence of a variety of opportunities or options. But in individualist accounts individuals require assets to realise these opportunities, otherwise they will be available only in theory, not in practice. Attention is paid especially to skills. In order for an individual to make effective choices, they require skills. Acquiring such assets is linked to responsibility. Personal responsibility is important for efficient selection of skills. Moreover resources are transferred to individuals in order to allow them to develop those features that promote effective choice. This then imposes obligations on individuals to make the best use of those resources. Contracts are often used to formalise these rights and obligations, but the use of contracts should not obscure the importance attached to individuals. Even those accounts in political philosophy that place contracts at the centre of their normative reasoning make, if implicitly, assumptions about individuals. The terms of any contract, for example, must be understood by individuals, raising questions about the nature of individuals. These questions can, however, be treated in a number of ways. One set of accounts may be built on free-market assumptions. Any contract here must be embedded within a wider social context. The importance of individuals is underlined by the fact that contracts are often devised on an individual basis. Rather than simply articulating a contract that applies uniformly across the whole society, one important theme is a focus on differentiated contracts. David Soskice, for example, in his account places particular emphasis on skills as a way of guaranteeing individual and collective economic success. Stakeholding involves a flexible contract between state and individual. Flexibility means that greater investment of effort or resources by individuals in the terms of the contract elicits greater rewards from the state. The focus is on individual investment nurtured by appropriate state encouragement. For some, if individuals were presented with attractive opportunities there would be no need to specify obligations since individuals would already have an incentive to accept these opportunities. Here, obligations are unnecessary. Obligations would only be required when opportunities are not sufficiently attractive for individuals to have an incentive to accept, in which case obligations are undesirable. The focus of these arguments is on the nature of opportunities facing individuals, rather than the resources used to ensure that these are real opportunities. It is this focus on resources that leads to an emphasis on obligation. Understood in this sense, stakeholding possesses instrumental dimensions, being a means to help promote autonomous choices. However knowledge and responsibility also possess intrinsic value for the stakeholder perspective.

With respect to skills, one strand of importance relates to the inculcation of entrepreneurial values. Here, ownership of welfare stakes helps to ensure that individuals will deploy these values in economically efficient ways. Alongside this is an emphasis on skills as a key factor of production within the context of the global economy. Individual learning accounts imply that individuals must be able to select and separate their own skills needs from those of other people. This points towards knowledge that develops largely in an individualistic context, and this covers certain species of technical and routine knowledge. This does not mean that these accounts cannot be applied to social skills, indeed one of the central motivations that Soskice has for these accounts is that he argues it will enable those at the intermediate and vocational educational level to acquire social skills, such as communication or presentational skills. In individualist models, skills tend to be emphasised for their contribution to a project of lifelong employability. Although some may regard entrepreneurial values and personal responsibility as overlapping concepts, personal responsibility and technical knowledge are distinct entities. As such, the distinction between responsibility and knowledge may be maintained. The focus on lifelong employability raises- the question of the extent to which these models of stakeholding are relevant for the retired. Since the retired have withdrawn from the labour market, policies for securing employment have little relevance. Similarly, those aspects of responsibility that are tied to a working life (a responsibility to invest in skills or one's pension) are not relevant for an individual once retired. While these sorts of development are not relevant, this does not mean stakeholding has no relevance at all for the retired. Certain stakes are not tied only to a working life, and as such are still relevant for the retired. Retired individuals could be shareholders in a company, or more generally involved in various institutions of civil society such as a credit union (an example of which is given in Chapter 4).

Tensions

As with collective models, the focus on responsibility and knowledge in individualist models is not without tension. With regard to ethics, personal responsibility can encourage introspection that hinders duties towards others. With regard to knowledge, certain skills are likely to be cumulative, building upon a particular set of skills to the exclusion of others. If an individual invests in an alternative set of skills at this earlier juncture, then the acquisition of these later skills will be precluded. Different skills, accordingly, cannot always be easily combined. A feature of stakeholding is an attempt to combine ideas from different realms (indeed, the separation of the economic realm from other realms is a notable source of criticism of orthodox economics from theorists of stakeholding); different approaches cannot always be easily combined since they are built on different assumptions and principles. For example, skills in the economic realm are largely understood in terms of efficiency. Responsibility is driven instead by ethical considerations. Although ethics and efficiency can be combined, they can also conflict. With regard to individual learning accounts, providing matching funds for individual contributions may introduce inefficiencies, through the distribution of risk associated with individual investment decisions. Individuals may be more tempted to make risky investments given that any investment will be partially subsidised than if they bear the full costs of any investments themselves. The distribution of capital may be better governed by economic than by ethical criteria. As with collectivist models, these difficulties do not mean that skills and responsibility cannot be usefully combined, but rather, that difficulties and trade-offs are likely to be faced.

Conclusion

This chapter has examined a second individualist strand of stakeholding, taking as its starting point the distribution of individual ownership within an economy and society. The purpose of the chapter has been to consider whether a coherent set of principles can be seen in the way in which individualist versions of stakeholding are constructed in Britain. To do this it has studied individualist arguments in the spheres of economics and welfare, drawing together common assumptions. It has argued that a coherent set of principles can be identified in terms of fostering responsibility and knowledge organised around the possession of stakes. As with the discussion of collectivist stakeholding, certain qualifications may be added. First, although the most developed accounts focus on individual responsibility and knowledge, alternative themes can also be detected. For example, some accounts of asset-based welfare simply highlight their contribution to a reduction in inequality (this being viewed as an end in itself). Not all accounts of asset-based strategies overlap with the approach set out here. Secondly, some simplification exists. A focus on common themes, for example, abstracts from differences between different theorists. As in the previous chapter, however, these differences are best seen within a common framework of individual responsibility and knowledge organised around the possession of stakes. Thirdly, for some of the theorists considered here, the themes associated with stakeholding do not represent an entirely new feature of their thought. Indeed, part of the reason for an attraction to stakeholding for these theorists is that it develops themes that they were already interested in. For example, character development was an important theme of Frank Field's thought before his advocacy of stakeholding. He was drawn to stakeholding because it allowed him to build on and develop these themes. This does not mean that stakeholding does not point in novel directions for such theorists. The focus on different forms of ownership for Field was a distinctive way of fostering his general agenda. Having surveyed collectivist and individualist accounts of stakeholding, the book now proceeds to examine the institutional and ownership context associated with stakeholding in greater depth.

4
Institutions and Ownership

This chapter widens the general discussion, arguing that stakeholding provides a distinctive and novel way of looking at civil society, the state and markets. Stakeholding puts emphasis on supporting a thriving civil society, such as churches, voluntary groups and self-help organisations. The state has a role to play in fostering diversity, for example using the law to protect building societies from pressures to demutualise. Markets have an undeniably important role to play in wealth creation in stakeholding, although this is fashioned in ways that try not to threaten social cohesion. The benefits and tensions that arise from the novel ways in which institutions are constructed in stakeholding are considered.

Stakeholding also breaks new ground with regard to ownership. Traditionally ownership discussions have revolved around private versus public property. In stakeholding this is replaced by a different notion of ownership that looks at the realm that exists between purely private and purely public property. This looks at the best mix of the rights and responsibilities of property – applying this to individuals and corporations. The ways in which property is distributed is also important, implying a significant restructuring of economic activity.

Collectivist institutions

Civil society

This chapter considers first the institutions associated with collectivist versions of stakeholding. After this, it explores the institutions linked to individualist approaches. Collectivist models of stakeholding intimate that individuals acquire responsibility and knowledge through contact with others. These models tend to imply that this occurs best when individuals interact with a small number of other individuals. This can be seen by noting the importance of long-term relationships in such models. Long-term relationships are not instantaneous; the implication is that a certain amount of time must be spent on a relationship. Since individuals have only a finite time at their disposal, they are able to engage in only a finite number of long-term relationships. It is likely that most individuals will only be able to engage in a small number of such relationships. Collectivist models tend also to emphasise that the acquisition of knowledge and responsibility occurs best when individuals are near to each other. This is because the costs of communicating information are generally reduced the nearer individuals are to each other. This is significant since the transfer of information provides an important foundation for the emergence of knowledge and responsibility. Combining a collective context with small-scale interactions points to the importance of institutions of civil society, understood broadly to refer to those intermediate organisations lying between the centre and individuals. Will Hutton and John Kay note that:

> [there] is a whole network of institutions that lie between the state and the individual – ranging from voluntary organizations and hospitals to quangos and firms. The insistence that our choice is either the state or the individual wholly neglects this institutional infrastructure and the importance of the social capital they generate. Rather the aim must be to nurture and sustain them. (Hutton and Kay 1996)

Emphasis is placed on 'bottom-up' or 'grassroots' organisations. These cover those small-scale collective bodies that inhabit the space between the individual and the state. Credit unions are an example of such bottom-up institutions. In a simple version of a credit union members come together each month and each places a fixed contribution into a central fund (which is kept in some form of bank account). This process is repeated at each of the successive monthly meetings. However, at each meeting one person makes a withdrawal from the fund. They are entitled to take a substantial portion of the funds saved (which typically far exceed their monthly contribution).

The person can then use this money however they wish. It might be used for home improvements, to pay for a holiday, or make some other type of financial investment. Each member of the group takes it in turn to make such a withdrawal (in rotation) at the regular meetings. The credit union, thus, is a society that enables individuals to have access to funds larger than those available had they saved on their own.

A particular conception of civil society is implied in collectivist accounts. Part of this emphasises the importance of pluralism. This draws attention to the wide variety of different lifestyles and life-choices. No single account of the good life can be imposed on these different lifestyles. Instead, there has to be acceptance of a variety of moral values. One feature of importance is that theorists are disposed to intervene, if necessary, to promote and protect diversity. The importance of this within a British context may be seen in debates relating to corporate governance. The public limited company (plc) form dominates the way in which large firms are organised in Britain. A plc is a shareholder model of the firm that has at least £50,000 in share capital, and where shares may be (though do not have to be) made available to the public. Theorists tend to emphasise, in a variety of ways, the importance of establishing conditions for the emergence of alternative organisational forms. Kay argues too,

> often it has been assumed that the only alternative to direct state ownership is the plc ... Even historically successful commercial organisations which are not plcs are finding themselves forced to adopt this mould because of a lack of adequate legal support for any other framework – as with mutual building societies and insurance companies, Lloyd's of London, and accountancy partnerships.
>
> (Kay 1996b, p. 43)

This emphasis arises, in part, from the belief that this will enhance efficiency. Paul Hirst has set out an important account of the link between diversity and efficiency. He argues that efficiency tends to be enhanced when economic decision-makers are close to the resources they manage. Gains accrue, for example, from a reduction in the costs of monitoring resources. This understanding points, within the context of a company, to a pluralistic governance structure. For Hirst, the complexity of economic activity means that it is unlikely that one type of governance structure will promote efficiency. Although some alternatives to the plc form may lead to inefficiency, there exist other forms that will foster efficiency. Within Britain there is a strong case for examining alternatives to the dominant public limited company (plc) form. This may require external intervention to address situations in which defenders of one type of governance structure are willing and able to prevent other forms from emerging (Hirst 1994). As an example of this Andrew Gamble and Gavin Kelly argue that there is a case for experimenting with alternative governance structures with respect to football clubs. They note that an increasing number of clubs have been floated on the stock exchange as plcs, and argue that fans 'believe big clubs are increasingly run in the interests of shareholders rather than supporters. To football fans, for whom transfer of loyalty is not an option, the trend is nothing short of a betrayal' (Gamble and Kelly 1998, p. 23). They argue that there are two broad strategies for helping to resolve these conflicts. First, a reformist corporate governance agenda tightening the accountability of directors while informally involving fans in various arenas. Though seen as an improvement, however, Gamble and Kelly regard this as insufficient to meet supporters' concerns. They emphasise, second, ownership changes. This could involve the widening of share-ownership among firms, or experimenting with 'mutual' ownership in which the fans become the club's members and legal owners.

Markets

Although collectivist accounts imply a prime focus on civil society, they also suggest that markets are likely to be important. Part of this emanates from moral commitments. Cooperation is less likely to emerge in a context in which there are few penalties for non-cooperation. On the one hand, those who are disposed to cooperate have little incentive to participate in committed relationships if they have few sanctions available should they be faced with hostile individuals. On the other hand, those who are disposed to behave non-cooperatively have little incentive not to do so if faced with few or no sanctions. Although a variety of sanctions may be constructed, the option of terminating a relationship through exit is likely to be important. Fashioning exit options implies a focus on market mechanisms. Although markets are likely to be important for fostering cooperation, in collectivist accounts they cannot be relied on alone to generate cooperation. This is because of the role given to commitment in helping to generate cooperation. Commitment opposes the emphasis on exit, therefore, pointing away from markets. Holtham and Kay suggest that markets can in fact undermine the moral foundations upon which market activity rests. In particular, individuals will only transact with one other if they can assume that everyone will generally stick to the agreed contract. Informational uncertainty means, however, that it is not possible to devise fully explicit contracts. Adherence to contracts here requires cooperation. But exit tends to drive out cooperation, related to the short-term nature of market-based relationships, and if exit can drive out cooperation, this ultimately hollows out the foundations upon which it depends for its existence. To prevent this, exit is likely to be curtailed. Indeed, for some, the emphasis on applying free markets to all areas of economic and social life has been dubbed 'market fundamentalism' (Gray 1997, p. 9). Alluding to religious fundamentalism, market fundamentalism is a pejorative phrase referring to the dogmatic and inflexible application of market principles irrespective of context and evidence of damaging consequences.

Markets are also important in collectivist accounts for efficiency reasons. Will Hutton and John Kay argue, 'Market organization, allowing the stimulus of competition, is the route to innovation and efficiency' (Hutton and Kay 1996). For these theorists competition within markets gives incentives (through the prospect, for example, of losing market share to competitors) for individuals to ensure that existing resources are deployed efficiently, as well as fostering the efficient development of new resources. Other properties of markets are also highlighted. Referring to markets, Hutton and Kay note, 'Decentralization of economic and political decision-making is more effective than the imposition of wisdom from the centre' (ibid.). For example, the centre faces problems in coordinating the mass of information that characterises economic activity. By minimising information requirements, markets in contrast help to achieve efficient coordination. There are nevertheless various efficiency limitations to markets. Part of this relates to conventional market failure arguments. Holtham and Kay argue that in certain cases markets may not exist. For example, the inability of insurers to monitor perfectly the behaviour of insured parties means that they often may be reluctant to offer full insurance. 'Moral hazard' problems emerge because insurers cannot ensure that individuals take the proper care to prevent the insured event from happening. As a result, insurers will be hesitant to offer full cover for such events. In areas such as health insurance, there may be gaps in the cover provided by the market. Insofar as such cover is thought important, there is a need for non-market intervention. Although non-market intervention can take a variety of forms, theorists of collectivist stakeholding pay attention to the role played by civil society.

Bottom-up institutions

The emphasis placed on fostering markets and developing non-statist collective institutions such as credit unions and supporter-owning football clubs points to the importance of 'bottom-up' institutions (that is, those locally based arenas for individual participation). This is not to suggest, however, that markets and civil society are easily reconciled. Inequality fostered by market interactions, for example, may hollow out a common space required for the flourishing of intermediate organisations. Some accounts may stress that one has to be tamed in favour of the other. Here any combination has to be weighted towards one or the other. Within collectivist models greater weight is placed on civil society given the emphasis on individual development through cooperative contact with others. There is a suggestion, however, in some quarters that changes in contemporary circumstances mean that it may be difficult to combine a liberal civil society with markets (Skidelsky 1996). This may fuel support for authoritarian or reactionary organisations. David Marquand notes: 'if the reborn social democrats betray the trust their electorates have placed in them, and fail to halt the growth of inequality, alienation and anomie against which their victories were a protest, a turn to darker forces could not be ruled out' (Marquand 1999b, p. 11). Although the failure of liberal civil society to contain any adverse consequences of markets may fuel reactionary movements, it is not clear that reactionary movements are better placed to succeed where liberal civil society fails. Both are seemingly subject to a fatalistic logic of the unfolding of markets. As Andrew Gamble points out, however, although fatalism is often associated with a deterministic logic, it is perhaps better understood in terms of contingency.

Although constraints are likely to be an important reality, there is also an opportunity for human agency to shape events within these constraints (Gamble 2000). On this understanding, even if the constraints imposed by markets are accepted, they can still be combined with a liberal civil society. In this case however the mix between markets and civil society may be shifted in favour of markets. These considerations mean that markets and civil society can be generally combined, although such a combination is unlikely to be free of tensions. Moreover, in certain circumstances only certain types of mix may be appropriate.

Top-down institutions

Although collectivist models display a bias towards bottom-up reform, the focus on civil society and markets does not imply that top-down institutions are unimportant. With regard to civil society, a central legal framework is crucial in helping promote diversity. John Parkinson for example has analysed how changes in company law can be used to promote pluralism within corporations. He advocates, in particular, setting directors' responsibilities so that they promote long-term relationships with a variety of stakeholders (Parkinson 1997a; 1997b). Also, without some collective agency which is able to remove potential obstacles placed by some groups in the path of others, giving priority to civil society may result simply in allowing certain groups to dominate others by virtue of enjoying greater resources. The centre is likely to possess important capabilities for removing obstacles, and as such can help promote a diverse civil society, as well as securing egalitarian commitments. Notwithstanding this there is a bias against the centre in much of the literature on stakeholding.

Certain top-down functions are likely to be performed, in a national context, by the state. For example, although supranational institutions are likely to play an important role in fashioning the legal framework, much of this is likely to be conducted through the state. However, the state can take on bottom-up forms. Although the state applies generally across society, it could devolve its functions to be performed by local institutions. Indeed, the state realm and civil society sometimes overlap (as, for example, with state churches). It is important within collectivist accounts to promote a non-state realm. Part of this relates to efficiency concerns.

Competition with non-state institutions, for example, helps assess the relative efficiency of state institutions. Also competition may occur with difficulty in a framework simply coordinated by the state. Ethical arguments are also raised regarding a non-state realm. For Holtham and Kay devolution of state functions has often led to losses in accountability. They argue that two solutions to this are commonly proffered, through the assertion of central political control or via contracts. They argue that the assertion of central political control is susceptible to an interest-group politics in which various groups will lobby the centre for favourable conditions in the setting of lines of accountability. They argue that it is unlikely that such interest-group politics will address concerns over democratic legitimacy, accountability here being dominated by particular groups rather than by decisions involving the whole community. The central difficulty with relying on contracts to set out accountability for these theorists is the general inability to write fully explicit contracts in an uncertain environment. In addition, even in those cases where explicit elements may be spelt out, the multifaceted, and often conflicting, nature of government objectives which characterises most policy areas means that it is difficult to capture these in a single contractual framework. Kay and Holtham argue instead for a non-statist system organised around three key elements. First, they note the importance of long-term relationships (or 'relational contracts'). This fosters the development of cooperation which helps deal with difficulties faced in articulating an explicit contractual framework. Second, supporting this involves the idea of an organisation as a 'trust'. Managers here see themeselves as 'trustees' of an organisation's mission to meeting the concerns of their stakeholders. For a firm this involves the idea, for example, of guaranteeing a certain level of customer care. Third, in order to secure accountability within these organisations they suggest a democratic framework in which stakeholders vote for a management board from a set of competitors at regular intervals. This helps, they argue, to satisfy conditions for accountability. Ian Harden and David Marquand's analysis of quasi-autonomous non-governmental organisations (quangos) has relevance for collectivist accounts of stakeholding (Harden and Marquand 1997). Quangos are organisations that perform governmental functions but are at arm's length from government. Quangos are important for Harden and Marquand in part because they improve the effectiveness of policy. This contribution to effectiveness may arise partly because they are separate from government. For example, Harden and Marquand note that an independent central bank charged with meeting an inflation target is often seen by financial actors as being able to make more credible policy commitments than government since it does not suffer the temptation to manipulate monetary policy for electoral or political reasons. Harden and Marquand also note the contribution that quangos can make towards participation. They note that individual participation need not be confined to electoral activity and that quangos can open up different types of participation. There is no reason why participation should be confined to the state realm. Indeed, the commitment to pluralism implies the existence of multiple sites of power that points to the importance of a non-state realm alongside any state realm.

Individualist institutions

Civil society

We now turn to a study of the role institutions play in individualist accounts. Individualist models point to an important role for civil society. Part of this emanates from efficiency concerns. Like theorists of collectivist stakeholding, individualist stakeholders have pointed to coordination failures associated with markets. This has been an important feature of Soskice's work, related to 'high skill, high quality' and 'low skill, low quality' equilibria in skills markets (Finegold and Soskice 1988). In particular, Finegold and Soskice suggest that Britain's poor record on intermediate vocational education and training might be explained by the fact that firms are trapped in a 'low skill, low quality' equilibrium. It is assumed that firms can choose to embark on either high or low quality product strategy, implying respectively a need for high or low quality workers. But even if a high quality route was deemed optimal, companies and individuals might not be able to break out from the 'low skill, low quality' equilibrium. Faced with low skill individuals, firms may have no incentive to employ a high quality product strategy. But employing this strategy would mean individuals have little incentive to acquire high skills, reinforcing the low quality product market strategy and so on. Shifting to the superior equilibrium would involve extra-market intervention. Tackling such coordination failures led to a focus on collective institutions. Moral considerations also point beyond markets. This is related in particular to the importance of duty. Markets are predicated on the assumption that individuals only act in accordance with self-interest. While duty may have a role for markets, insofar as markets help constitute incentives in those areas in which self-interest and duty coincide, this means that executing obligations points beyond a market ethic.

The emphasis on collective institutions in stakeholding approaches utilises civil society rather than the state. This originates, in part, from difficulties perceived in fashioning social capital in a centralised context. From a game-theoretic perspective, for example, if the payoffs from cooperation are divided in proportion to the number of players in a game (but the payoffs from defection remain relatively constant), then as the number of players in a game are increased, the incentive to cooperate is progressively diminished. This means that coordination is more difficult to achieve in a centralised context. The focus on efficiency prioritises certain institutions. In the context of welfare this leads to a focus on self-help and friendly societies. Combining a focus on self-help with an emphasis on the importance of ownership leads has led to a focus on mutuals. Here recipients of welfare have ownership stakes in welfare providers. With regard to social capital, one institution that has attracted general attention relates to rotating credit associations described above.

Markets

Individualist accounts place greater weight than collectivist accounts on markets. The emphasis upon choice within individualist accounts points to an important role for markets since they foster individual choice. By allowing individuals to make choices, markets permit those inequalities rooted in differential preferences (which are generally regarded as just) to emerge. This does not imply a focus on unfettered markets however. Although markets permit inequalities rooted in choice, unfettered markets also permit inequalities rooted in brute luck to emerge. Unfettered markets enable the naturally talented to command a higher wage than the less talented. Similarly, those with greater material endowments through lucky family circumstances can often translate existing inequalities into future inequalities (by affording greater investment opportunities, enhancing bargaining positions and so on). Helping address brute luck inequality points to some intervention within markets.

On an efficiency level, an important focus of individualist models is on skills that can be articulated in an explicit format. It is feasible that such skills can be transferred via markets. It is plausible to suggest that this will also be desirable. Gary Becker suggested that efficient acquisition of skills is best conducted through markets. In particular, he argued that efficient acquisition of skills occurs when its benefits exceed its costs. He contends that individuals can trap most of the benefits of skills, and they are accordingly best placed to know when the benefits of any investment exceed its costs. If costs are borne elsewhere, however, individuals would have an incentive just to focus on the benefits (rather than, as efficiency dictates, both costs and benefits). Becker argued that to foster efficiency, individuals should bear the costs of skills acquisition. These cost–benefit calculations are best conducted through markets (Becker 1964). Becker formed an important efficiency rationale for the use of markets for skills acquisition. The importance of these arguments has been accepted in this broad tradition (Layard 1997). This does not mean that there has been uncritical acceptance of Becker's ideas. Paul Chapman highlights general concerns when he notes that problems may arise if individuals are not fully informed about the benefits of any investment, or are capital-constrained and so cannot bear its costs (Chapman 1998). It is plausible to suggest that policies such as individual learning accounts may improve the functioning of markets in these instances. By making individuals bear some of the costs of investment, a link is still made between benefits and costs. External finance could help tackle any credit-rationing faced by individuals. A quality control on modules for sale may help improve the information available to individuals. Although for Becker efficiency demands that individuals bear the full weight of any costs, lack of access to capital or uncertainty about benefits means that this 'first best' is unlikely to be achieved in practice. Efficiency is likely to involve 'second best' policies of the sort considered here.

Top-down institutions

The above discussion does not mean that the centre is unimportant. It is important, for example, in a regulatory capacity. Ensuring that individuals execute their duties implies that, should individuals fail to respond to incentives and so on, they are simply forced to fulfil those duties. The success of this approach implies the existence of an external agent with sufficient coercive capabilities to perform this task. In a national context this is likely to involve the state. The centre is also important in a distributive capacity, in helping to ensure that all individuals have access to endowments. Furthermore, this implies that it has some investment functions manifested in policies such as individual learning accounts. Greater importance is attached, nevertheless, to a non-state context. This can be seen with respect, for example, to welfare. State intervention can occur on several levels, relating to funding, provision and regulation. With regard to welfare, the state could finance it, provide it through state agencies and regulate all intervention. However, while these different functions have often been conflated in post-war welfare, they are separable. For example, the state could provide and finance welfare, but rely simply on private finance. Alternatively, it could fund a service, but contract out to non-state providers. Field has advocated uncoupling these different functions and exploring the possibility that certain functions may be performed by non-state agencies. Part of this focus emanates from recognition that the state is unlikely to act in ways it once could, given changes in the global economy. These changes stress that governance is not interchangeable with government, but that it involves a range of non-state institutions, an important set of which inhabits civil society. Part of this emanates from the importance given to promoting a pluralistic politics, which here involves promoting multiple sites of power. For Field, it is important to have such institutions to check, and if necessary oppose, the state.

Ownership

This chapter now considers a particularly important type of stake in stakeholder accounts, namely ownership. Within individualist strains of stakeholding this is seen in the preponderance of proposals related to individual ownership, such as individual learning accounts, stakeholder pensions and employee share-ownership. Within collectivist accounts, the attention paid to the governance of firms and public services often raises issues of ownership. As David Marquand argues, 'At the heart of the stakeholder concept lies the simple proposition that Property must discharge obligations to the wider community as well as to its owners: that the decisions of a capitalist firm must reflect the interests of its employees, its suppliers and the localities in which it operates as well as those of its shareholders' (Marquand 1996). This is not to say that all contributors to collectivist accounts refer to the importance of ownership at all times. For example, John Kay has raised some doubts about the usefulness of applying the concept of ownership to certain aspects of a stakeholder analysis of firms. Discussing the sorts of networks that help constitute a firm's resources, he says:

> It is difficult to see how the concept of ownership – analogous to ownership of an umbrella – could be relevant. What could we mean by the ownership of a set of routines, or a structure of relationships? You can benefit from the returns they generate, but that is not at all the same as owning them. If anyone did own these things, it is more likely to be the employees than the shareholders. But they do not really own them either. We are talking about things to which the concept of ownership simply does not apply, like friendship, or conservatism, or tennis.
>
> (Kay 1997a, p. 131)

This does not mean that Kay regards ownership as irrelevant. He accepts, for example, that individuals have property rights over shares in a firm. However, he suggests that some aspects of a firm are not amenable to ownership. Some have criticised this latter stance. Ruth Levitas, for example, argues that,

> the claim that ownership is unimportant, that it does not matter who owns the firm, and that no-one really does, is more than a quirky observation. Its effect is that the marked social division between those who own the bulk of productive wealth and those who do not mysteriously disappears. If there is no ownership, there is no ownership class either. Capitalism is a set of relationships; but the very relationship which characterizes it is obliterated from view.
>
> (Levitas 1998, p. 74)

Kay does not suggest, however, that rights and responsibilities cannot be applied over firms at all. Indeed, his view of a firm as a 'trust' in which managers have to discharge obligations points to the importance of such an agenda. Rather, he suggests that these are not *ownership* rights. The sorts of rights and responsibilities associated with a trust, however, do seem, against Kay, to raise issues of corporate property, even if Kay is reluctant to use the concept in this area himself. So even for those who raise doubts about the usefulness of applying the concept of ownership in all cases, their suggested alternatives often seem in practice to inhabit very similar terrain. As such, even in such situations a study of ownership is valuable.

Forms of property

Collectivist models of stakeholding emphasise the fostering of individual responsibility and knowledge through contact with others. Helping promote responsibility and knowledge here points to an important role for articulating the obligations of property. But to provide incentives this is combined with an agenda that also asserts the rights of property. This indicates attention paid to the form of ownership, that is the appropriate mix of rights and responsibilities of property. This is based on the recognition that ownership is a multifaceted concept, and that different combinations of these facets yield different property forms. A. M. Honore argued, for instance, that eleven main elements typically define ownership across space and time, namely characteristics related to possession, use, management, income, capital value, security from expropriation, transmission, freehold, duty not to harm, judgemental liability and residual control of an entity. Different mixes of these elements lead to different models of ownership. Considering what is meant by ownership of a simple item such as an umbrella helps illustrate the different facets of ownership that Honore draws attention to. The first facet of the right of possession means that individuals can insist on holding the umbrella for themselves. Secondly, the right to use implies that individuals are free to use an umbrella however they choose. Typically, this involves individuals putting it up once it is raining (though it does not have to be used only in this particular way). Third, the right to manage involves the owner's right to manage how others use the umbrella. If the owner lends the umbrella to a friend, he or she can ask that the borrower shakes off any rainwater before closing the umbrella. The fourth dimension, of right to income, means that the owner has the right to any income generated from the use of the umbrella (for example to the money they may charge for lending the umbrella to others). The fifth element, of right to capital value, implies that if a person sells the umbrella, he or she is entitled to keep the proceeds from the sale. The right to security from expropriation concerns, sixthly, the right an owner has to protection from theft. If someone takes the umbrella without the owner's consent, the owner is entitled to report this as a theft to the police and demand that their property be recovered. The seventh characteristic, of right to transmission, covers the right of an owner to transmit the umbrella to others. A person is allowed to sell the umbrella, give it as a present or leave it in a bequest. The eighth right, concerning freehold, means that there is no time limit on any of the rights that an owner exercises. The ninth aspect encompasses the duty of owners not to harm others by using the umbrella to cause physical injury. The tenth characteristic, of judgement liability, means that the owner of the umbrella is liable for any legal action taken with respect to the umbrella. The right to residual control implies, lastly, that the person resumes all those rights of ownership they confer to borrowers once the period of the loan has elapsed (Honore 1961).

This agenda forms one of the main ways ownership has been treated in collectivist stakeholder accounts. It has featured in areas such as corporate governance in the United States and elsewhere since at least the 1960s. Historically this reformist tradition was subsumed by the wider debate on ownership. In particular, for much of the twentieth century, ownership debates were presented as a choice between either pure private or full common ownership where all rights were bundled in private or common hands respectively. At least two qualifications may be added to this characterisation. First, there were always exceptions to the stark choice between private and common property regimes. Private property based regimes usually had some role for common ownership, through cooperatives or state ownership of natural monopolies for example, and common ownership regimes allowed for the private ownership of certain consumption goods. Second, the choice was not simply between pure private or common property. Private ownership did not typically confer unfettered rights: most regimes incorporated, to varying degrees, obligations in terms of payment of tax, for example. Similarly, with regard to common ownership, some rights over any surplus generated were permitted to allow for incentives for optimal economic activity for managers of state-owned enterprises in common property regimes. In spite of these qualifications, debates were dominated nonetheless by a basic choice between pure private or common ownership regimes.

A focus on 'hybrid' property raises questions, however, regarding the connection between stakeholding and capitalism. In particular, most theorists of stakeholding in Britain suggest that their proposals amount to an endorsement of stakeholder capitalism. But hybrid property maps out a space inhabited by both hybrid private and common property. The boundary between private and common ownership forms may be quantitative (where property is deemed private or common to the extent to which the majority of rights are held in private or common hands respectively), qualitative (where property is private or common depending on whether specific rights are placed in private or common hands), or some combination of these. Given this, if capitalism or socialism is taken to refer to regimes in which there is a majority of private or common forms respectively, then stakeholding may be developed either in capitalist or socialist directions. Any connection between stakeholding and capitalism here is not necessary, but contingent. In spite of this, theorists of hybrid models in Britain may be justified in referring to stakeholder capitalism since they have developed proposals within the context of British property relations, which are predominantly capitalist. The majority of hybrid property forms are private hybrid forms.

An important caveat to this in collectivist accounts are the moves made to develop new forms of common property. Although there is broad acceptance of the failure of the specific ownership forms associated with state socialism, this has not been translated into a wholesale rejection of all types of collective ownership. Like private ownership, collective property can be constructed in a variety of ways. Some attention has been paid to fashioning alternative models of common property. Gerald Holtham outlines an important example of this. Holtham argues that public ownership may be a useful tool for attaining various policy objectives. He says that within Britain there are important elements of consumption that are arranged collectively. He draws particular attention to the realms of health and education. These are free to all at the point of delivery. A central issue concerns how such services are financed. He argues that the rate of growth of these sectors is greater than the rate of growth of gross domestic product. This means that if the state were to finance increases in health and education through the taxation system, then this would imply a higher tax burden on individuals. He suggests that common ownership offers an attractive alternative. He claims that this provides a way of financing greater expenditure without a higher tax burden. He contends, in particular, that the average rate of return on shares invested on the stock market outstrips the rates of growth of gross domestic product, health and education. He says that if funds could be invested on the stock market, then this would furnish a 'community fund' from which spending on health and education could be financed. Here, stakeholding 'may have to mean that the community, not as individuals but the community collectively, has a stake in national wealth and uses it to underpin those elements of consumption, which it also wishes to arrange collectively' (Holtham 1997, p. 8). He contests that taking receipts from the closing of tax loopholes as well as one-off increases in corporation tax and merger activity would generate the initial funds for investment. City investors would then manage this fund. Once established this scheme would be self-financing. Holtham argues that such a scheme is already functioning in Singapore, and could be usefully deployed in Britain. Although initiatives such as these do not alter the bias towards private property forms in Britain, they do highlight that collective forms are important notwithstanding this bias.

The distribution of property

The individualist emphasis on the acquisition of responsibility and knowledge apart from other things points to the importance of spreading individual ownership. This looks at distributive issues, in particular how individual ownership is spread across a population. As Frank Field argues, stakeholding is in an important sense the 'child of the early postwar drive towards a property-owning and shareholding democracy' (Field 1996b). This agenda is the main way that ownership is treated in individualist stakeholding. A variety of justifications have been given for individual ownership in this tradition. One set of arguments is based on efficiency considerations. For some, individual ownership is conducive to the formation of a private knowledge resource that may be used to realise efficiency benefits. Incentive arguments stress how individual ownership helps provide individuals with appropriate incentives for optimal economic activity. Ethical arguments have also been important for the plural tradition. Some models suggest, for example, that individual ownership is necessary for securing equality. Insofar as individual ownership is stressed, this points towards a capitalist doctrine.

Conclusion

This chapter has considered the institutional and ownership implications of a stakeholder approach. Much of this encompasses the sorts of stakes used within stakeholding to promote the acquisition of responsibility and skills. In relation to institutions it has contended that while the state has a role to play in both collectivist and individualist accounts, there is a common emphasis in stakeholding on a 'bottom-up' context organised around some mix of civil society and markets. It has been suggested that within this framework collectivist models give greater weight to civil society and individualist accounts to markets. Ownership is a particularly important type of stake in stakeholding. Two broad ownership agendas have been identified. One looks at the form of property relations, that is, the rights and responsibilities of ownership. The other is a distributive agenda that focuses on spreading individual ownership across society. The chapter has noted that collectivist models are more closely associated with the 'hybrid' agenda, while individualist versions are linked more strongly to the distributive agenda.

Now that the institutional and ownership implications of stakeholding have been considered, this chapter has concluded the examination of the different elements that constitute collectivist and individualist stakeholding. The next chapter moves on to consider whether stakeholding thus understood furnishes a viable set of third-way principles.

5 Criticisms and Combinations

Up to now this book has concentrated on setting out and exploring two of the main strands of stakeholder theory, namely, collectivist and individualist stakeholding. After considering each of these components in turn, the book has looked at the general ownership and institutional issues connected with stakeholding. Having covered this ground, this chapter focuses on two main issues. The first part of the chapter contemplates the extent to which stakeholding forms a coherent alternative to Keynesian social democracy and free markets suited to contemporary conditions. This is the central question posed on stakeholding in this book. This is addressed by breaking down the central question into several components. Namely, to what extent is stakeholding coherent; to what extent is it an alternative to Keynesian social democracy and free markets; and finally to what extent is it feasible in a global context? Each of these questions is asked of collectivist and individualist accounts of stakeholding in turn.

This chapter contends that stakeholding does furnish a coherent set of principles; that such principles are distinct from Keynesian social democracy and free markets; and that they are feasible in modern conditions. Thus stakeholding does in fact furnish a coherent set of principles that break from old politics and are feasible in modern circumstances. This underlines that stakeholding is an interesting perspective in public policy and is worthy of further development. The differences between recent attempts on the left and right to chart third ways are recorded to show the distinctiveness of the stakeholder position. Secondly, it considers the ways in which collectivist and individualist strands overlap and combine. Although it is valuable for analytical reasons to separate our collectivist and individualist accounts, it is also important to note that in a significant set of cases elements of these different components of stakeholding are combined with each other. For example, Frank Field advocates using mutual organisations as the main delivery mechanism for his proposals on stakeholder pensions. The second part of this chapter studies some of the ways in which collectivist and individualist currents intertwine, as well as the tensions and the trade-offs that are linked to this.

Coherence

Stakeholding faced a host of criticisms when it first emerged. Some alleged it was incoherent – that stakeholding did not represent a consistent set of principles, being marked instead by contradictions. Others claimed that it did not break with the policies previously adopted by either Labour or the Conservatives. These critics said that for all its claims to novelty, stakeholding was simply a version of Keynesian social democracy or (for other critics) free markets. Still others said that it could not be made to work in modern circumstances. This meant that even if stakeholding was coherent and did represent something new, it was not viable in contemporary circumstances. Though distinct, each of these criticisms denies the importance of stakeholding as a new and interesting way of looking at public policy. These criticisms are challenged here, with the argument that stakeholding is a more subtle and robust set of ideas than many of its detractors contended. Many of the critics did not concentrate their fire on the strongest accounts of stakeholding.

With respect to collectivist models, charges of incoherence are usually expressed in relation to corporate governance. Elaine Sternberg expresses many of these criticisms. For Sternberg the 'term "stakeholder" is popularly associated with three conflicting doctrines, two commonplace and the other largely incoherent' (Sternberg 1998, p. 94). Sternberg contends that stakeholding forms a distinctive approach through its injunction to replace any specific organisational objectives with the aim simply to balance stakeholder benefits. She argues that this injunction leads to a series of definitional problems. Managers, Sternberg argues, face problems pinpointing who shall count as stakeholders. In principle, she contends, the list could be endless. This is likely to mean that managers will be embarked on a time-consuming and never-ending task of identifying stakeholders. On top of this there are problems of deciding what counts as benefits for different stakeholders. Different stakeholders are likely to enjoy different benefits. It is difficult, however, for managers to calculate the benefits for different stakeholders. Even if this were resolved, there would be a problem of balancing out different benefits. There are problems in deciding if some benefits should take priority and, if so, what their relative weight should be. Although Sternberg accepts that these difficulties may be avoided by referring to some overriding organisational objective, she argues that this possibility is not open for stakeholders since the commitment simply to balance stakeholder benefits rules this out. With respect to firms, this means that stakeholding will replace the shareholder system of accountability, in which managers are only accountable to shareholders, with an unworkable alternative.

She argues that it is important to firmly resist this conception of stakeholding. On the one hand, Sternberg argues that stakeholding undermines notions of rights over property, such as owners being able to dispose of property in any way they choose. Given that organisational property is seen as the central foundation for other property forms, this means stakeholding will undermine the foundation of all private property. Against the counter argument that property rights are typically qualified (in obligations to pay tax, for example) Sternberg states that this is not a reason for further extending constraints on property. Moreover stakeholding denies that managers have duties to shareholders. These issues are important for Sternberg since the above are deemed central to well-functioning economic activity and individual liberty. Although Sternberg rejects an approach based on balancing stakeholder benefits, she does not suggest dispensing with stakeholding entirely. She argues that it can be deployed in two useful ways. First, as a convenient label reminding us that the success of a firm often depends upon engagement with stakeholders. Secondly, it serves to remind individuals that insofar as they have an impact on company business, they have a responsibility to convey any concerns to managers in a conscientious manner. However, these are commonplace, not novel, understandings for Sternberg. Thus she concludes that insofar as stakeholding is useful, it is not new, and insofar as it is distinctive, it is unworkable.

Response

The purpose of the conception of stakeholding outlined here is not to support an ill-defined notion of balancing stakeholder benefits (that is to deny the importance of any specific organisational objectives). A focus on cooperative relationships offers a narrower understanding of stakeholding than that implied by a policy of balancing stakeholder benefits. Although this criterion is not perhaps as narrow as one that distributes ownership to those who supply financial capital, it nevertheless clearly identifies important stakeholders such as workers, suppliers and consumers. Cooperation is more likely to occur when people are close to each other (the costs of monitoring defection are lower), so stakeholders are those proximate to each other, ruling out those that are further afield from a firm. Although claims for recognition from those denied stakeholder status may still emerge, they are unlikely to be appreciably greater than those that arise from critics of shareholder governance. Sternberg's view that stakeholding undermines managerial duties is at odds with the fact that many theorists of stakeholding endorse the idea of a stakeholder charter, where managers fulfil certain stated responsibilities. It seems relatively easy to devise governance structures that include employees as well as those that contribute financial capital. Kay offers the example of 'customer corporations', where governance is altered to allow consumer representation in certain privatised utilities such as water (Kay 1996b). The limitations faced in extending governance to some stakeholders should not act as a deterrent to alter governance where this is possible. This understanding of stakeholding, however, does not rob it of its distinctive content. In particular, although the idea that the profitability of a firm depends upon successful engagement with stakeholders is not novel, the particular emphasis placed on examining the internal architecture and the role of ownership is new. Stakeholding here is not merely a label or a reminder to individuals to act conscientiously, rather it implies institutional change. This is not intended however to undermine a private property-based regime. John Plender, for example, sets his account explicitly against the failure of the socialist case for undermining private property. Indeed, his focus on spreading ownership intends to widen the benefits of private property. Attention is focused thus on its distribution, as well as on what the various rights and responsibilities of property are. The focus on responsibility is not without limit, or justified simply on the basis of existing obligations. Any focus on responsibility is constrained by the importance attached to the rights of property, as well as being directed to helping promote skills.

Gerald Holtham offers an important justification for such a position (Holtham 1997), and similar justifications are given by Margaret Blair (Blair 1995). For Holtham, one important argument justifying shareholder claims is that since shareholders bear risk for the success or otherwise of the firm in light of their financial capital invested, they have legitimate claims over the managers of the corporation. The basis of this legitimacy lies in the risk borne by these individuals. Gerald Holtham argues however that it is difficult to see why this criterion only applies to shareholders. He argues that individual workers also bear risk when they have to make firm-specific skills investments. In fact, he suggests that the risk borne by workers may exceed that of shareholders. Shareholders are able in particular to diversify risk in their individual share portfolios in ways unavailable to individual workers. This points to a situation in which any justification for shareholder concerns are likely to apply also for other stakeholders. More generally, given the contribution of both shareholders and non-shareholders towards business, for stakeholders it is difficult to see why attention should be confined to shareholder concerns alone.

Incompatible with liberal precepts?

Although individualist models of stakeholding are not usually viewed as incoherent, it is alleged that they are incompatible with liberal assumptions (which is a source of worry given the weight placed on such notions). Desmond King and Mark Wickham-Jones suggest that the emphasis on balancing rights with responsibilities in policies such as welfare-to-work in fact represents a break in the liberal precepts of British social democracy. Rights with responsibilities are regarded as incompatible with a philosophy of social rights. Here it is suggested that rights are necessarily unconditional, whereas rights and responsibilities violate this by making rights dependent on the exercise of some condition(s) (King and Wickham-Jones 1999). Stuart White argues however that this view is flawed. To show this he draws a distinction between,

> (1) a right to be given some resource, X, unconditionally; and (2) an unconditional right of reasonable access to a given resource, X, where reasonable access means, in part, that the resource in question can be acquired and enjoyed and by the individual concerned without unreasonable effort.
>
> (White 2000, p. 510)

White argues that an individual can have reasonable access to something, without being given this thing directly. He suggests for example that providing an individual with ingredients, a recipe, a cooker and relevant utensils, means that this person has reasonable access to a particular meal, even though they have not been given the meal itself. Rights of the second sort, he argues, are an important theme of centre-left traditions. He quotes L. T. Hobhouse who noted,

> the function of the State is to secure conditions upon which its citizens are able to win by their own efforts all that is necessary to a full civic efficiency. It is not for the State to feed, house, or clothe them. It is for the State to take care that the economic conditions are such that the normal man who is not defective in mind or body or will can by useful labour feed, house, and clothe himself and his family ... [In this sense] 'right to work' and the right to a 'living wage' are just as valid as the rights of person and property.
>
> (Hobhouse 1911, p. 76)

Similar themes, he argues, are found in T. H. Marshall, R. H. Tawney and Harold Laski. For White, the emphasis on responsibility emanates from the importance of a reciprocity principle. Here 'those who willingly share in the economic benefits of social co-operation have a corresponding obligation to make, if so able, a personal and relevantly proportional productive contribution to the community in return for these benefits' (White 1999, p. 168). From a social democratic perspective, however, White argues that any attachment to reciprocity must be supplemented by two other commitments. First, a commitment to ensure fair reciprocity. This means that individuals are faced with real opportunities, which implies for White equal access to those resources that underpin opportunities. Secondly, a respect for individual autonomy. White draws attention to the importance of John Stuart Mill's 'harm principle', that intervention should only be licensed where individual conduct causes significant harm to others. White argues that, on this basis, some criticisms may be directed at Labour since it has intervened in certain areas (related to the family, for example) in which there has been little violation of the harm principle. Nevertheless for White matching rights and responsibilities is compatible with the invocation of the harm principle, and accordingly some interventions by Labour on this basis may be justified. Obligations here serve to prevent 'a specific form of harm – the economic exploitation that arises when one citizen opts to free-ride, and so unfairly curtail the economic opportunities of, his or her fellow citizens' (White 1999, p. 174). Following White, the discourse of matching rights and responsibilities can be defended from a social democratic perspective, given a commitment also to real opportunities and individual autonomy.

Nick Ellison suggests that the thrust of stakeholder welfare may be unpractical (Ellison 1998). He argues that a statist model of welfare has been eschewed, and there is a greater emphasis on the private sector to provide the opportunities for the individual welfare recipients. However the private sector may not perform this task, either because it is not able to (in a recession, say), does not want to (there is little individual incentive to do so) or both. Given that the state has withdrawn from welfare provision this may mean, particularly in bad economic times (which are precisely the times at which welfare policy is critical), welfarism will not function properly. Ellison's critique assumes the straightforward replacement of state with private sector (in particular corporate) provision. Although it is true that stakeholding implies a bottom-up political project, this does not mean, as we have seen, that the role of the state is unimportant. Furthermore Ellison believes that a statist system of welfare is increasingly difficult to sustain within the global economy (though he laments this). He does not, however, articulate an alternative model of welfare. Nevertheless, it is possible that stakeholding, with its redefined role for the state, may in fact ultimately address some of Ellison's concerns.

Third way

Alternative to free markets

As we have seen, stakeholder models imply a bottom-up context organised around a mix of civil society and markets. The departure from free markets is clearest with respect to collectivist models. Here greater emphasis is placed on civil society than on markets, either as a complement to or as a means of controlling market activity. Some indication of this is provided by the intensity of criticism expressed by committed supporters of free markets, such as Elaine Sternberg, against stakeholder corporate governance. She firmly rejects, as seen above, any intervention within markets to secure stakeholder objectives. Individualist models are closer to free markets insofar as greater weight is given to markets than to civil society. Nevertheless individualist models are not a version of free markets. First, they do not see markets as the sole organising principle of economic and social life. This leads theorists of individualist models to emphasise the role of collective institutions. Second, the conception of markets in individualist accounts differs from those of advocates of free markets. Attention is placed on ensuring that individuals have real opportunities in markets through a focus on assets. This centrally involves individuals' knowledge development. The focus on responsibility alongside real opportunity also points beyond a market ethic. Third, the state has a more extensive role than implied in free-market accounts. The state does not simply aim to remove barriers and help to police market activity as in free-market accounts. In individualist accounts the state actively intervenes in market processes.

It may be objected instead that stakeholding relies too heavily on questions that free markets raise, notwithstanding the fact that this reformism offers different answers. For example, David Coates suggests that much reformism amounts to ensuring that labour acquire those characteristics suited to capital (typically by improving the quality of labour through investment in skills, or enhancing flexibility) while leaving capital untouched (Coates 2000). The focus on responsibility might be seen, on this view, as simply a convenient discourse to legitimate improvements in the quality of labour useful for unfettered capital. This is important for Coates since most of the problems of capitalism are rooted in capital, not labour, and he argues that greater emphasis should be placed on tackling problems associated with capital. For Coates this implies the replacement of capitalism with socialism. Although theorists of stakeholding do consider the questions that free marketeers raise to be important, they do not confine themselves to answering only free-market questions. In particular, attention is paid to the nature and distribution of capital in an economy. This points to an interventionist agenda that no supporter of free markets would countenance. One strand to this focuses on equality, paying attention to issues such as ensuring that all individuals have an equality of endowments (that allows the opportunities all individuals face to be real rather than formal). With regard to skills acquisition, this has focused on policies such as individual learning accounts. A second strand focuses on altering the constitution of companies to go beyond shareholder concerns. Any reform of corporations is important since they are (for some, the most) important institutions within a capitalist economy. Coates is sceptical, however, of all reformist strategies. Regardless of whether or not these reformist ideas are capable of resolving the problems Coates identifies with capitalism, they cannot be said to be only interested in the questions that free marketeers pose.

Alternative to Keynesian social democracy

Stakeholding is differentiated from Keynesian social democracy mainly through its emphasis on bottom-up reform. Although bottom-up elements were present in Keynesian social democracy, this public policy framework primarily relied on top-down state intervention guided in accordance with Keynesian economic principles. This contrasts with the greater stress on civil society and markets within stakeholder accounts. Although collectivist strands of stakeholding agree with Keynesian social democrats about the need for collectivist intervention, the main focus of attention is on corporations, voluntary organisations and cooperative societies rather than the state. Individualist models of stakeholding go beyond Keynesian social democracy in highlighting the role of individual responsibility and markets. While a focus on duty was an important part of T. H. Marshall's concept of social rights, individualist accounts of stakeholding arguably go further in balancing the rights and responsibilities of individuals. Greater weight is also placed on shifting attention away from the state towards the market.

Feasibility

Having argued that collectivist and individualist strains of stakeholding constitute a coherent set of third-way principles, this chapter now considers the extent to which they are viable in contemporary conditions. An important part of this concerns stakeholding in relation to globalisation. Some individuals underline the importance of stakeholding regardless of any assessments made about changes in the global economy. For example, John Kay argues that:

> [despite] the internationalisation of markets, despite air travel, despite information technology, there are still things that are done best by people who find themselves frequently in the same room. The most important of these are the transfer of skills and knowledge and the development of trust between individuals. It is on success in creating networks that facilitate these exchanges that many competitive advantages in today's world depend.
>
> (Kay 1996d, p. 74)

For Kay, this conception provides a basis for national competitive advantage. Kay's argument resonates, in part, with Michael Porter's analysis of the competitive advantage of nations (Porter 1990). Taking the view that it is ultimately firms, not nations, that compete, Porter argues that discussions of national competitiveness should concentrate on examining the ways in which the national context can provide the conditions in which firms can thrive (by fostering, for example, a legal framework conducive to corporate success). Firms are understood to derive their competitive advantage largely from the way in which they tie together different aspects of their operations. Government policy can help foster this by creating a framework conducive to the combination of different elements that constitute firms' competitive advantage. Kay contends that the theory of comparative advantage predicts that trade reflects differential endowments of natural resources. In a nation, specialisation occurs in those areas in which a higher endowment of natural resources relative to other nations is enjoyed. He argues, though, that this fails to explain the structure of trade where natural resources are broadly similar (which defines much of economic activity), as well as the fact that specialisation occurs in areas in which there is no apparent endowment of natural resources. Modern trade theory, he argues, has instead developed accounts couched in scale economies and imperfect competition. He contends that this explains the fact, rather than the structure, of trade. In contrast he suggests that the resource-based view of the firm better explains national competitive advantage.

The development of specific organisational capabilities helps to define activity in particular sectors, which then forms the basis for national competitive advantage. This view also helps explain why successful economic activity is often geographically concentrated.

A different view places more weight on considering stakeholding in the light of global economic changes. The view here is that global economic changes have altered the terrain of public policy, and it is important, accordingly, to consider stakeholding from this perspective. Collectivist models of the sort endorsed by Kay are likely to be important for this understanding of the significance of these global economic changes. One significant aspect of such models of global economic activity is the impetus that changes give to pluralism. Here local communities develop distinct resources from commitment as a way of responding to global economic imperatives ('thinking global, but acting local'). Though important, it is unlikely however that collectivist models will be sufficient on their own to meet such imperatives. Although their emphasis on commitment is significant, it is also probable that flexibility in responding to changed circumstances will be important. Here individualist models, with their focus on transferable skills, are likely to be important. Relying only on individualist models, however, downplays the importance of the specific and tacit skills born of a collectivist approach. Generally speaking, combining commitment and flexibility implies that the optimal stakeholder model in the light of global economic changes is likely to involve some mix of collectivist and individualist approaches, rather than relying on ideal types. Similarly, with regard to confronting pluralism, the emphasis on choice within individualist accounts is likely to be important for allowing the existence of different lifestyles. But this must be placed alongside the continued importance of common bonds, which points in collectivist directions. Furthermore, although markets allowing different people to pursue different ends means that markets can *prima facie* accommodate individuals with different identities, they are ill suited to dealing with pluralism. This is because markets rely on the assumption that values can be subject to comparison, which implies the existence of a common standard (typically money). As with economic changes, this means that the optimal model is likely to involve both individualist and collectivist approaches. That is not to say that all the problems associated with globalisation will be resolved simply. Rather, stakeholding is likely to be viable in a global context, and the optimal configuration is likely to involve both collectivist and individualist elements.

Although important, globalisation is not the only significant issue to consider when studying the viability of stakeholding in contemporary conditions. A common emphasis (though modelled in different ways) in collectivist and individualist accounts of stakeholding is the stress on promoting the individual acquisition of knowledge and responsibility organised around the possession of stakes. For this to be viable individuals must be capable of developing responsible forms of behaviour and skills. The feasibility, and limits, of development is therefore an important question for collectivist and individualist stakeholding. This question has tended to attract little explicit attention within stakeholder discourse. Most stakeholder accounts assume that individuals are capable of behaving responsibly and acquiring skills. This derives, in part, from the emphasis given to innate capacities. This is most clearly evident with regard to knowledge dimensions. Implicit in the emphasis on individual learning accounts is the assumption that all individuals have some innate capacity to develop, else there is little justification for distributing learning accounts in this manner. This does not imply that individuals are all equally talented, or that they are all talented in the same area. Indeed, that learning accounts allow different individuals to acquire different skills is in part a recognition of the fact that individuals are differentially talented and should be permitted to acquire those skills to which they are best suited. It is usually assumed that innate natural talents are distributed arbitrarily by nature. Innate capacities are also important in collectivist accounts. Mutual education emphasises how humans have limited capabilities, which provides a basic justification for learning, negotiation and persuasion among similarly placed individuals. This implies that individuals are malleable and capable of altering their views. Although tied in most obviously with knowledge, innate capacities are also important when considering responsibility. While these models do not usually suggest that all individuals are able to develop equally, it is generally assumed that individuals are capable of developing some basic threshold level of appropriate virtues. An emphasis on non-innate capacities complements this. Non-innate capacities relate to knowledge or ethical characteristics that are the result of social construction. With respect to ethics, this is highlighted by the importance given to mutual obligation, with respect to knowledge with the idea of social skills. Although innate capacities might still be important here in the sense, for example, that some individuals might be more disposed to develop social skills than others, communication within a group must allow the least able to engage with others.

Notwithstanding the above, certain individuals may be unable both to acquire skills and to behave responsibly. In some cases, individuals may be able to acquire skills but not behave responsibly, or alternatively, to behave responsibly but be unable to develop skills. Young children, for example, may be able to acquire skills through early learning, but may often be unable to assume responsibility for their own actions. Conversely, certain categories of the mentally disabled may be able to act responsibly but be unable to acquire skills. An important issue concerns the treatment of such individuals. This may be tackled, in certain instances, by allowing other individuals to assume the complementary emphasis. This applies, in particular, to children and responsibility. Parents or guardians here may have to display responsibilities for their child's education. This strategy is more relevant for individualist than collectivist models. In collectivist models, where responsibility occurs through interactions with others, parents or guardians cannot adopt this role for their children. This is more relevant for individualist models, where obligation is centred more closely on individuals. However, there are likely to be constraints regarding the extent to which parents or guardians can properly identify the appropriate skills needs of their children. Where it is not possible to support these complementary emphases elsewhere, stakeholders are likely to promote whatever acquisition of knowledge or responsibility is possible. In some cases individuals are unlikely to display either knowledge or responsibility. This covers certain categories of sick or disabled individuals. In these instances, theorists tend to distribute according to need.

Third way alternatives

It is the contention of the above that stakeholding does in fact provide a coherent set of principles of public policy that differ from Keynesian social democracy and free markets. Moreover, they are viable in modern conditions. This answers the main question posed of stakeholder theory: namely, whether it constitutes a feasible third way. This should not be understood as saying that the whole of the third-way space can be understood in terms of stakeholding. The space between Keynesian social democracy and free markets is compatible with a range of projects, and only part of this is described by stakeholding. In spite of a range mapped out by individualist and collectivist models, stakeholding can be distinguished from other projects that inhabit third-way space. To highlight some of the distinctiveness of the stakeholder position, we now compare stakeholding to projects on right and left. Associative democracy is a related project on the left. Paul Hirst is an important contemporary exponent. For Hirst, associative democracy is underpinned by three key principles. First, collective organisations or associations within civil society are the main mechanism for promoting democracy in the economy and society. Secondly, a principle of subsidiarity in which power is distributed to the lowest level that is consistent with the execution of these affairs. Power should always be devolved to the lowest level at which it can still be carried out properly. Thirdly, a focus on democracy as communication. Rather than focusing on democracy as adding up existing preferences of voters, stress is given to the shaping and transforming of preferences through discussion and debate. These elements are in fact interlinked. Associative democracy focuses centrally on the extension of democratic principles across economy and society. Democracy is understood in terms of communication, and for Hirst, such communication is best realised through associations. Individuals must however be able to structure public policy choices if these deliberations are to have real influence. In order to maximise opportunities for such influence, Hirst advocates distributing power at the lowest level consistent with the proper execution of any stipulated tasks (Hirst 1994). Associative democracy overlaps most closely with collectivist models of stakeholding (though Hirst's advocacy of a basic income grant as part of his proposals intersects with individualist concerns). The focus on civil society is the most obvious overlap. In this regard Hirst has referred to stakeholder notions in relation to corporate governance. In spite of these overlaps, there are important differences between stakeholding and associative democracy. First, the central purpose of associative democracy relates to the extension of democratic ideas, whereas stakeholding is more narrowly focused on responsibility and knowledge. Greater focus is also made, second, on knowledge development within stakeholding. Although Hirst has some knowledge elements in his notion of democracy, other theorists of stakeholding focus on broader skills issues. Lastly, stakeholding can be developed in a more narrowly individualistic fashion. For example, in individualist models of stakeholding greater weight is given to development within the context of markets, than to associations. This indicates a space beyond any concerns of associative democracy.

Civic conservatism

Civic conservatism is a related project on the right. David Willetts best captures the contours of this. Civic conservatism places the 'free market in the context of institutions and values which make up civil society' (Willetts 1997, p. 94). For Willetts, civic conservatism aims to negotiate a broader tension at the heart of much political theory, that is the tension between 'the anonymous structure of transactions and rules in a modern free-market society ... and ... the close ties of community where understandings do not have to be explicit because they are so deeply shared' (ibid., p. 169). He argues that the market and the community capture what most individuals regard as important in their lives. The market is important for Willetts for its contribution to prosperity and freedom. He argues that markets harness both the instinct to better oneself (which promotes work, saving and investment), and the instinct to truck, barter and exchange. These are central, Willetts argues, for producing individual and collective prosperity. In addition, markets are an essential component of freedom, allowing individuals to make unconstrained choices. For Willetts, however, simply relying on the market is not sufficient to deliver the good society. He argues individuals also desire a society with 'thick social ties, not one which has been finely graded into individual grains moving frictionlessly past each other' (ibid., p. 168). In fact, values

> ranging from particular virtues, like honesty and fairness, through to ties of affinity to the wider community, constrain the market. The values are sustained by non-market institutions that help to shape our behaviour. And the free market actually needs these values in order to operate: they provide the cultural and moral environment it needs.
>
> (Ibid., p. 90)

He claims both of these themes have been important historically in conservative traditions. He argues that a common error is to regard the market as a threat to, and the state as a protector of, civil society. On the one hand the market is not a threat to civil society since efficient market activity often relies on cooperation. Markets act as a mechanism bringing diverse individuals more closely together, many of whom conjoin in institutions of civil society. On the other hand, the state is destructive since it simply substitutes top-down state provision for any provision by the institutions of civil society. State expansion, for example, has undermined the working-class self-help organisations such as 'friendly societies, mechanics institutes and local guilds' (ibid., p. 93). The challenge identified by Willetts instead is to develop such collective institutions. This understanding of civic conservatism occupies essentially the same terrain as collectivist models of stakeholding and associative democracy. Responsibility is also an important part of Willetts' proposals. The focus above is on how individuals may be shaped by their local environment. In areas such as welfare, he argues that we 'also have to accept, whether we like or not that the welfare state inevitably has an impact on people's behaviour and that we have to think about what these impacts may be' (ibid., p. 126). Willetts also draws attention to the role of duty. He notes, 'One way in which conservatives have tied their commitment to property rights and a market economy into a wider ethical scheme has been through an appeal to Christian duty' (ibid., p. 170). Willetts notes the importance of duty. He notes that duty has, historically, been conducted through an appeal to the Christian faith. He argues however that in an increasingly secular society such appeals have less resonance. Given the continued importance of duty, the task therefore is to develop new accounts that are suitable for modern society.

Although there are significant overlaps, it is important to distinguish civic conservatism from stakeholding. Willetts' criticisms of intervention to secure diverse corporate governance forms have already been noted. More importantly he claims that the 'intellectual battleground between conservatives and socialists is over economic inequality, differences in income and wealth' (Willetts 1992, p. 111). For conservatives, pursuit of equality is 'wrong in principle' (ibid., p. 113). This sets Willetts most obviously against the importance of reducing inequalities of outcome for theorists of stakeholding. He also rejects any arguments for endowment equality. He notes that left thinkers attempt to justify equality in terms of helping promote liberty. He argues that this approach follows the basic structure that 'freedom really means practical opportunities to shape and control one's own life; socialist egalitarianism means spreading these practical opportunities as widely as possible; egalitarianism therefore means maximizing freedom' (ibid., pp. 115–16). But, for Willetts, the free market is the best way of spreading opportunities. This means accepting the importance of inequality since inequality is an essential part of free-market logic. He argues the 'free-market system, which so powerfully spreads these opportunities, needs disparities of income and wealth in order to function' (ibid., p. 117). Focusing on equality would be counterproductive since this would require a concentration of state power which represents 'an enormous loss of opportunities to control one's own life' (ibid.).

Combination

Having contended that stakeholding constitutes a viable set of third-way principles, this chapter now looks at ways in which these different strands of stakeholding are intertwined. It was noted above that an effective response to global changes is likely to involve elements of both collectivist and individualist stakeholding. This points to the importance of blending together the different strands of stakeholding and this in fact occurs at a number of junctures. Although there are real differences between collectivist and individualist accounts, there are important overlaps. A core assumption held in common between the collectivist and individualist accounts of stakeholding is the importance attached to 'responsible individualism'. This stress on responsibility springs from a shared reaction against unbridled or free-market individualism. Frank Field, Will Hutton, John Kay, John Gray and David Marquand emphasised that they,

> repudiate this economic individualism and its associated political philosophy absolutely. Above all, we believe it to be a gross misunderstanding of what really drives a market economy and wealth creation ... All markets are social and political as well as economic. They are made to work by *real* people embedded in a *real* culture, interacting in *real* institutions.
>
> (Field et al. 1996)

These thinkers stress the network of ties and duties linking individuals to each other. Free-market individualism ignores the importance of such ties. This attachment carries a number of implications. It involves a repudiation of the dominant model of individuals in modern economics. This model of 'rational economic man' is closely tied to free-market individualism. John Kay argues 'we are fundamentally social creatures. We do not have concepts of justice of rationality, or indeed preferences, formed independently of the social environment within which we operate' (Kay 1997b, p. 7). Kay argues that this was recognised in classical economic thought, particularly by Adam Smith. Kay argues that Smith is a misunderstood figure in much of orthodox economic analysis. In particular, he argues that many economists infer from *An Enquiry into the Nature and Causes of the Wealth of Nations* that Smith supported a model of the self that was later to be formalised as rational economic man (Smith 1993). However, Kay argues that this neglects the importance that Smith attached to mutual sympathy, and more generally his moral philosophy, as set out in *The Theory of Moral Sentiments* (Smith 1976). For Kay, Smith had a view that extended beyond rational economic man. Whatever the reasons for this neglect, Kay represents himself as a direct heir of such thought and seeks to reinvigorate an important, but neglected, economic tradition. The critique of rational economic man here takes on another dimension, but not only is it an inappropriate model, it is also based upon a false reading of the economic traditions upon which this is ostensibly built.

The focus on duty and obligation in individualist accounts points in similar directions. Fulfilling obligations, in at least some instances, is likely to be counter to a person's rational self-interest. Amartya Sen's distinction between sympathy and commitment helps illustrate this. Sen distinguishes between two sorts of altruism, namely sympathy and commitment. He claims that sympathy 'corresponds to the case in which the concern for others directly affects one's own welfare' (Sen 1990, p. 31). However, commitment involves 'a person choosing an act that he believes will yield a lower level of personal welfare to him than an alternative that is also available to him' (ibid., p. 32). Such committed behaviour might arise, for instance, from the demands of a personal morality. 'Sympathetic altruism' is essentially self-interested altruism. However Sen notes that 'commitment altruism' is often an important part of human motivation. Any incorporation of altruism into rational economic man is bound to be incomplete since this will necessarily rule out commitment altruism.

The central problem with equating cooperation with sympathetic altruism is that its success depends (using game theory as an illustrative context) upon a suitably constructed repeated game. If, however, the nature of the game suddenly alters owing to environmental change, there is no guarantee that cooperation will continually form the best strategy. Defection might now be best. Continued cooperation here is more likely to be grounded in genuinely committed, rather than sympathetic, motivations. Environmental change, in particular informational uncertainty and flux, is precisely the situation trust is intended to deal with. But this is the situation where the parameters of any game are likely to alter. Thus there are grounds to suggest that, insofar as such cases are important for stakeholding, cooperation must extend beyond sympathetic altruism to cover commitment altruism. Charles Leadbeater notes, 'Trust and co-operation are as critical to success in the modern economy as self-interest' (Leadbeater 2000, p. 150). This is not to say that rational self-interest is unimportant (indeed individual ownership is stressed in part for the individual incentives it provides), but that stakeholding helps inculcate a sense of mutual trust.

Theorists of stakeholding also have common cause in rejecting models of responsibility that emerge from the right. The criticisms that centre-left theorists levelled at free-market individualism do not transfer straightforwardly to neoconservative prescriptions. This latter individualism does not ignore the importance of communal ties, which is seen in the criticisms of a dependency culture by right-wing thinkers such as Lawrence Mead. For Mead it was precisely the lack of recognition that individuals have duties towards themselves and their families that led to many welfare problems (Mead 1986). Such accounts were influential for thinkers such as Frank Field. But this does not mean that centre-left theorists accepted the prescriptions offered by the right. Greater emphasis was placed on providing individuals with equal endowments within left rather than right accounts. That is, centre-left accounts place greater emphasis than those of the right on the idea that resources have to be distributed more equally across society if all individuals are to have access to the resources they need to flourish properly. Accordingly, differences existed over the treatment of equality. Moreover, concerns over dependency existed alongside an emphasis on the importance of fostering a sense of cooperation and trust in left accounts. This looks beyond issues of personal responsibility, at how cooperation may be fostered in a collective context.

There are also important cases where individuals tie together the institutional and ownership mechanisms associated with collectivist and individualist approaches. For instance, Andrew Gamble and Gavin Kelly weld together collectivist and individualist approaches to ownership in their discussion of stakeholding. Their project is driven by the belief that an 'egalitarian market economy should be the foundation of left political economy' (Gamble and Kelly 1996a, p. 64). Although the continuing importance of public ownership is accepted, Gamble and Kelly argue it is more important to 'develop a distinctive approach to private ownership' (ibid., p. 63). They reject the idea that this simply represents capitulation to a New Right agenda, arguing instead that ownership issues are too important to be surrendered to the Right. Ethically, they argue that ownership of private assets is an increasingly significant determinant of the distribution of income and wealth within society (with inequalities of income and wealth still being regarded by most egalitarians as key indicators of the state of equality within society). With regard to efficiency, developments in information economics point to the importance of the pattern of endowments. Small amounts of wealth, for example, may help individuals overcome credit rationing wrought by informational deficiencies and promote investment in skills and be a spur to entrepreneurial activity. But it is important, they argue, to consider the different facets of ownership. They note:

> pure forms of ownership, however, are a rarity in modern economics. They are only found in relation to the most simple objects. All other property rights are limited and qualified, and the bundle of different rights involved in ownership have become increasingly separated and assigned to different agents.
>
> (Gamble and Kelly 1996a, p. 72)

This is important because exploring this space of different combinations of the rights and responsibilities of ownership points to the construction of new forms of private ownership. It also points, however, to the importance of spreading ownership. An 'egalitarian strategy must involve both redistribution of property rights and the exercise of the rights and ownership' (ibid., p. 82). They contend that this has developed mainly along either liberal egalitarian or socialist lines. Liberal egalitarians, they argue, have focused on policies such as labour–capital partnerships within firms, and socialists are currently focusing on market socialism. The main problem with the liberal egalitarian tradition is that it 'contains little discussion of the realm of the political, either of the political feasibility of its proposals or of the role of non-market institutions' (ibid., p. 79). Gamble and Kelly contend that a key strength of market socialism is the importance attached to collective mechanisms in helping to implement proposals. They reject the case for market socialism, however, arguing that it does not offer anything more that a private property regime, and that its socialism has become formal. As an example of the new ownership agenda they consider the importance of stakeholding. Here 'stakeholding revives and restates crucial elements of the traditional social-democratic agenda' (ibid., p. 80). Stakeholder capitalism, they argue, has two main themes. The first is an idea of inclusion 'that citizens acquire a stake in society by giving them opportunities and rights to participate through programmes which deliver employment, welfare and education' (ibid.). The second theme, concerning mechanisms to achieve these aims, focuses on reforms to corporate governance. Reform of corporate governance, they argue, would serve two main objectives: as a way of improving economic performance, and as a step towards economic democracy (Gamble and Kelly 1996b). Elsewhere Charles Leadbeater, for example, has shifted onto some of the terrain that he earlier criticised. In particular, he has considered some reforms of corporate governance along collectivist stakeholder lines alongside his advocacy of individualist stakeholding. This is seen in his analysis of 'know-how' firms. He argues that while the traditional company is based on an assertion of shareholder rights, the 'know-how firm is created when property rights are pooled, by a social contract among peers, not by the top-down delegation of power from shareholders to managers' (Leadbeater 2000, p. 177). He says this points to new forms of hybrid corporate property.

Tensions

Though collectivist and individualist strands of stakeholding can be combined, this is not entirely free of tensions. For example, tensions exist in relation to combining the different ownership agendas.

In corporate governance emphasis is placed on spreading ownership stakes as well as looking at the rights and responsibilities of property owners. This focus on the form and distribution of property is not without tension. Form emphasises the obligations of property owners. Obligations are intended in important part to promote activity. Within the context of a firm, this could involve workers being actively involved in joint consultative committees. Distributing property may place obstacles in the path of activity. Spreading ownership may lead to 'free-rider' problems. While individuals may bear the cost of any personal intervention, widening ownership means that the benefits of intervention are shared generally. Individuals may have an incentive to free-ride on others. If all individuals free-ride, interventions to improve the condition of property owners will not occur. Fostering activity here means placing less emphasis on dispersing property (so that the benefits of intervention are less generally shared). This is not to say that form and distribution cannot be combined, only that in an important set of cases this is likely to involve trade-offs.

Tensions also exist in the differing institutional mixes favoured in individualist and collectivist approaches. Although both approaches prioritise bottom-up institutions involving both markets and civil society, individualist and collectivist approaches are weighted towards markets and civil society respectively. Here they point in differing directions, which means that combining collectivist and individualist approaches implies that trade-offs will have to be confronted.

Conclusion

This chapter has concentrated on two main issues. The first part has argued that stakeholding furnishes a set of principles to reform public policy that differ from a reliance on free markets or Keynesian social democracy that are also viable in modern circumstances. In order to show this the chapter has had to draw on the material on collectivist and individualist strands of stakeholding set out and explored in earlier chapters. It has argued that each of these strands of stakeholding is robust to a variety of criticisms that deny that stakeholding amounts to a third way. The chapter pulls together, therefore, the various threads connected with the first main claim of this book, that stakeholding provides the centre-left with a feasible set of third-way policy reforms. This issue is important because such an agenda is thought to be crucial for any renewal of the centre-left. The second part of this chapter has examined the ways in which the different strands of stakeholding overlap and combine. This is driven by recognition that while it is valuable for analytical reasons to separate out the different versions of stakeholding, in a substantial set of cases these different components intertwine. Some of the tensions and trade-offs that this throws up has been the subject of discussion.

Having completed the case for the first main claim of this book, the next chapter moves to consider the second major claim, that is, stakeholding remains important for understanding New Labour ideas and policy. As noted in the introductory chapter, stakeholding originally acquired political importance when Tony Blair said that it would help fashion New Labour's project in office. This bolstered the significance of stakeholding since it promised to have practical consequences for the organisation of the British economy and society alongside its impact in intellectual debates. But as the introductory chapter also notes, this promise seemed to evaporate very quickly. This, at least, is a view common to much of the commentary on the relationship between stakeholding and New Labour. By studying New Labour thought and policy, the next chapter rejects this view. While stakeholding has been scaled down, an important set of the ideas and policies of New Labour overlap with stakeholding. It is not that stakeholding has had a lingering death, but rather that New Labour has picked up and developed themes associated with individualist and collectivist stakeholding. Recognising this is important for underlining the practical impact of stakeholding but also for gaining a fuller understanding of the character of New Labour.

6
Stakeholding and New Labour

There is much contention surrounding the idea of New Labour. A significant part of this suggests that style rather than substance dominates New Labour. Here, it is said that New Labour reformers only pay attention to getting elected to government, ditching whatever policies are thought to hamper this. This has meant an obsession with focus groups, opinion polling and spin (Bayley 1999). Although such electoral considerations are undeniably important for any party seeking office, this chapter suggests that to see New Labour only in these terms is inadequate. It fails to recognise the substantial agenda which is involved in New Labour. This chapter argues that one of the unique and significant elements of New Labour is the influence of stakeholding on its thinking. While the explicit attention to stakeholding as an overall organising project proved to be brief, many of the themes underpinning it have survived into subsequent third-way discourse. Also, there are at the present time significant policy moves in stakeholder directions. This is not to say that ideas simply dictate policy in a straightforward manner. Ideas are only one of the factors that impinge on policy (others include personalities and unforeseen events). Moreover, the unfolding of policy can feed back and help fashion theoretical debates. In spite of these qualifications, it is contended that New Labour's policy approach has substance, and overlaps importantly with stakeholder themes.

Discourse

Any analysis of New Labour discourse has, however, to confront several problems. First, some of the writing surrounding New Labour is expressed in general terms. Steve Ludlam argues, for example, that Peter Mandelson and Roger Liddle's understanding of ethical socialism is couched in terms so general that it would be uncontroversial in most political philosophies. This creates a problem for identifying a distinct set of ideas (Ludlam 2000). Second, at times some of this discourse is of a confused or contradictory character. David Marquand, for example, contends that Blair presents no clear and consistent ideology (Marquand 2001). Third, part of New Labour discourse is self-serving. Here, part of the identity of New Labour comes from misrepresenting the nature of 'old Labour'. It also exaggerates its own novelty and importance. This complicates the task of separating the true shape of any ideology from the rhetoric. All these considerations make the task of identifying a precise conception in New Labour discourse more difficult. Although important, these considerations do not mean that a core cannot be identified at all. Indeed, given the time and effort expended by politicians and intellectuals, it would be surprising if nothing at all could be detected. Although this discourse does display generalities it has, with passing time, begun to centre on important themes. Also, even if some individuals display confusion, this does not imply that all individuals do so. Indeed, Marquand argues that some coherence can be detected in New Labour's welfare reform programme. It is difficult for such coherence to emerge without some consistency at the level of ideas. Moreover, there is also debate over whether some individuals are as confused as they are sometimes presented as being. For example, Martin Smith and Mike Kenny argue that Marquand underestimates the role played by ethical socialism for Blair's thought (Kenny and Smith 2001). Raymond Plant similarly sees coherence in Blair's thought, analysing this within a brand of revisionist social democracy (Plant 2001). Lastly, although old Labour may be misrepresented and the novelty of New Labour exaggerated, this does not mean that New Labour cannot be seen in distinctive or novel terms. As such, an examination of New Labour discourse, notwithstanding the above considerations, is of some value. I now proceed to examine, with these qualifications in mind, the discourse surrounding New Labour.

Collectivist stakeholding

Stakeholding played an important role in New Labour discourse. Interest was signalled by a high-profile speech that Tony Blair made to the Singapore business community in 1996, and by positive statements made by other individuals closely connected with New Labour. In his speeches on stakeholding, Blair argued that the stakeholder economy implied a core emphasis upon '"investment", "quality" and "trust"'(Blair 1996, p. 291). He mapped out two possible futures for the British economy. One future focuses on creating a large number of goods that can be sold cheaply. Such a strategy favours the production of low-quality commodities. Such goods favour processes that involve a large number of unskilled workers. Even if the low-quality route was thought desirable, Blair argued that it was not feasible, since this would involve competing with countries, many of them newly developing, where labour costs were much lower. Given that the low-quality route relied mainly on unskilled workers, this meant that companies in Britain would effectively be unable to compete with such companies elsewhere. This left the high-quality route. The second future is to create a small number of goods that can be sold at high prices. This involves the production of high-quality goods. These commodities imply extensive use of sophisticated technology and equipment. This points to the importance of a highly trained workforce, and means a central emphasis on the acquisition of skills. Any help provided to individuals in relation to acquiring those skills associated with a high-quality route had to be combined with a stress on balancing rights with responsibilities:

> Above all, however, we must create a society based on a notion of mutual rights and responsibilities, on what is actually a modern notion of social justice – 'something for something'. We accept our duty as a society to give each person a stake in its future. And in return each person accepts responsibility to respond, to work to improve themselves.
>
> (Blair 1996, p. 298)

An important part of discussions of stakeholding paid attention to collectivist models. These were expressed primarily in relation to corporate governance. Blair's speech engendered a positive response from trade unionists. John Monks, the Secretary General of the Trades Union Congress (TUC), noted that 'Stakeholding is an exciting idea which has emerged as the unregulated, free-market excesses of the 1980s are in their death throes' (Monks 1996). Although Monks denied that stakeholding represented a return to previous models of corporatism, he did see it as implying an important role for unions. Monks contended that,

> Tony Blair's stakeholder philosophy reminds us that the basic stakeholder is the individual. Each individual employee has a stake in the success of his or her company, and in the prosperity and opportunities this should bring. Independent unions are the means for individuals to exercise their voices or to realise their stakes collectively, and thus more effectively.
>
> (Monks 1996)

John Edmonds, the leader of the General, Municipal and Boilermakers union, on BBC Radio's *World at One* programme on 17 January 1996 similarly supported stakeholding, stating also that 'there will be even more need under a stakeholder economy for trade union support to ensure their rights are properly implemented' (quoted in Webster and Sherman 1996). Janet Williamson, a Policy Officer at the TUC and a member of the TUC's Stakeholder Task Group set out an important part of the TUC's agenda (Williamson 1997; 1996). Williamson argues that the current system of corporate governance is characterised by the sort of managerial short-termism identified by Will Hutton in Chapter 2 above. Managers are pressurised by financial markets to divert resources in order to pay high dividends to shareholders. Although Williamson argues that shareholders are important, companies 'affect and are affected by a far wider range of groups than just shareholders – at the heart of every company is a web of stakeholder relationships, each of which is based on mutual dependence' (Williamson 1997, p. 158). These cooperative relationships are central, it is suggested, for promoting efficiency. Measures should be taken to institutionalise stakeholder concerns, and a variety of mechanisms are advocated within this context. One relates to enhanced reporting requirements. Each 'individual company should therefore monitor and report on its particular stakeholder relationships in the same way as each monitors and reports on its financial health' (Williamson 1997, p. 160). A second tool involves using directors' responsibilities to specify the duties owed to constituent stakeholders. A central role for trade unions is identified in promoting a stakeholder conception of firms. Williamson contends that trade unions 'have been representing the collective interests of workers for the past 150 years, and it is in this capacity that they have a crucial role to play in supporting stakeholding in the workplace. Trade unions provide a natural mechanism through which employee voice can be effectively represented for the purposes of consultation as well as negotiation' (Williamson 1997, p. 165).

Individualist stakeholding

Individualist models of stakeholding were also a feature of the debates surrounding stakeholding. Peter Mandelson and Roger Liddle saw stakeholding as addressing the 'needs and aspirations of individuals, not interest groups acting for them' (Mandelson and Liddle 1996, p. 25). Similarly Alistair Darling conceives of stakeholding as a philosophy for individuals. Two themes inform both accounts. One central theme relates to individual opportunity. For Darling, individuals 'should have the opportunity to contribute, to be allowed to do the best they can for themselves and their families' (Darling 1997, p. 10). A focus on opportunity is important for both economic efficiency and social cohesion. Lack of opportunity to work, for example, for Darling imposes various economic costs in terms of unemployment as well as undermining social cohesion through the exclusion of the unemployed from society, so hollowing out a common arena in which mutual bonds may be formed. Mandelson and Liddle note however that individuals 'cannot reach their full potential alone, and nor will the "free" market ensure it either. They need the opportunities that come from being part of a strong community that acts together to back up their efforts' (Mandelson and Liddle 1996, p. 20). This is 'at the heart of the stakeholder economy New Labour wishes to create' (ibid., p. 19). Emphasis is placed on the provision of skills. Darling notes that government 'has a duty to ensure that people have access to the best possible education ... High quality education and training are essential, not just at the start of life, but throughout life' (Darling 1997, p. 14). Mandelson and Liddle note 'the potential of national economic policy is not so much reduced as narrowed in scope. Governments can still take action to enhance skills, promote investment, and enlarge our economic capacity to strengthen the so-called supply-side' (Mandelson and Liddle 1996, p. 6). The second theme for these thinkers relates to the importance of responsibility. Mandelson and Liddle argue that 'rights carry with them obligations' (ibid., p. 20). Similarly, Darling notes there 'is a contract, or understanding, between the individual and the government: the individual will expect the government to put in place a framework and the opportunities for education; in turn they have a responsibility to take up that assistance and make the most of those opportunities' (Darling 1997, p. 15). Darling underlines the importance of individual ownership for helping to underpin this general agenda. Within corporate governance he argues it

> is crucial that individuals who work in a business have a stake in its future so that they feel committed and identify with the enterprise with which they are involved. Successful companies see their employees as a resource not just of production but often as a source of creative innovation... Employee-share ownership, for example, can play a major role in providing motivation and incentives of individuals to work'. (Ibid., p. 19)

In order to foster real opportunity and responsibility, attention is drawn to the role played by the individual ownership of stakes.

Third way

As noted in Chapter 1, New Labour interest in stakeholding attracted fierce criticisms from the right. Following these criticisms, New Labour retreated from referring to stakeholding as an organising project. The attachment to stakeholding was replaced by references to the third way. The third way is supposed to be an alternative to 'old' Labour and free markets. The third way is subject to a variety of criticisms. One important set of concerns relates to whether any coherence can be detected within the third way. I wish to suggest that a coherent conception can be identified. In this chapter attention is paid specifically to overlaps with a stakeholder agenda, not suggesting that this is a complete account of the third way, but simply arguing that the third way is not empty, and that an important strand within it overlaps with the accounts of stakeholding set out in this book.

The stress on knowledge and responsibility in stakeholding is a continuing theme of the third way. Tony Blair and German Chancellor Gerhard Schroeder argue that the 'top priority must be investment in human and social capital' (Blair and Schroeder 1999, p. 6). For Blair and Schroeder investment in skills is important, however, for helping to ensure that the opportunities an individual faces are real rather than purely formal. Respecting the equal worth of all individuals means focusing on skills policies for all individuals, not simply a select few. Although economic policy makes extensive use of markets, this does not reflect a free-market conception. Markets are not unfettered, rather non-market intervention is important for ensuring that all market participants have relevant levels of skills. This non-market intervention implied an important role for the community, in terms for example of securing the transfer of resources in order to help foster skills acquisition. This, however, imposed reciprocal obligations on individuals towards the community. The emphasis on community and obligation was manifested with a focus on matching rights with responsibilities. Similar themes can be detected in the statements of other important contributors to the third way. For example Anthony Giddens, an academic close to Tony Blair, noted, 'One might suggest as a prime motto for the new politics, *no rights without responsibilities*' (Giddens 1998, p. 65). Emphasis is placed on inculcating responsibility, and this is mediated largely by stressing responsibilities as well as rights. The doctrine of real opportunity points towards the acquisition of skills. Giddens argues, the 'guideline is investment in *human capital* wherever possible, rather than the direct provision of economic maintenance' (ibid., p. 117).

Collectivist models

There are a variety of ways of fostering responsibility and knowledge. Not all of these point in stakeholder directions. But an important set of mechanisms in the third way do point towards stakeholding, in part drawing attention to the importance of collectivist models. Tony Blair argues:

> [The] third way recognises the limits of government in the social sphere, but also the need for government within those limits, to forge new partnerships with the voluntary sector. Whether in education, health, social work, crime prevention or the care of children, 'enabling' government strengthens civil society rather than weakening it, and helps families and communities improve their own performance.
>
> (Blair 1998, p. 14)

Many of the critiques of government intervention are thought important by supporters of the third way. Emphasis is placed, accordingly, on other types of institution. The attention paid to responsibility is thought to imply the significance of a public realm, pointing, for advocates of the third way, to the need for public institutions. Public bodies do not have to be identified solely with government, and stress is placed on fostering non-governmental organisations such as voluntary societies and community groups, these falling within the broad remit of 'civil society'. The attention paid to civil society leads to a focus on some form of government intervention, notwithstanding the limits imposed on it. Government has a role in helping to fashion civil society, for example, by instituting a legal framework conducive to the emergence of a variety of forms of organisation. Another salient feature of the third way is acceptance that this may involve a role for the private sector, in both delivery and in funding. Blair argues that without core values, 'we are adrift. But in giving them practical effect, a large measure of pragmatism is essential. As I say continually, what matters is what works to give effect to our values' (ibid., p. 4). This means that there is no ideological bar to the use of private bodies, where these can be used to help promote the funding or delivery of services. Any use of private bodies is circumscribed, however, by the significance attached to creating a public realm. As such, there are boundaries imposed on the privatisation of education.

Themes from collectivist stakeholding also surface in discussions of 'public service corporations' or 'pluralist' models of the firm. John Kay maintains that reform of public services such as education and health are at the top of the domestic political agenda. He suggests that the 'most important problem that Labour faces in its second term concerns the management of these public services' (Kay 2001, p. 10). Reform should be driven by the attachment to 'disciplined pluralism' that involves 'processes of diverse experiment, audit and accountability' (ibid., p. 11). He states that the 'key requirement is to define and refine the British model of what we might call the public service corporations. Public service corporations cover activities as diverse as water supply, rail services, airport management, museums, hospitals and universities' (ibid.). Repeating the sort of reforms he advocated of corporate governance, he says the governance of public service corporations 'must itself entrench pluralism. The supervisory board should be representative of a range of interests. But it should act as a board, rather than as representatives of these interests' (ibid.).

He also draws attention to the significance of widening reporting requirements and having a diversity of organisational forms. Gavin Kelly and John Parkinson repeat stakeholder themes in their discussion of the pluralist foundations of the company. They note that the traditional view of corporations insists that shareholders should be seen as the sole owners of a firm since they are the residual bearers of risk. While not denying the importance of linking governance to risk, or the significance of shareholders in relation to this, Kelly and Parkinson argue that 'if there is a plurality of groups who are exposed to residual risk, then this should be reflected in how corporate objectives are formulated and in the design of corporate governance structures' (Kelly and Parkinson 2001, p. 113). Echoing the position of Gerald Holtham and Margaret Blair outlined earlier, they contend that this situation does in fact characterise firms. There is a case for integrating stakeholders such as employees and customers in the governance structures of firms. They consider ways of improving participation (such as securing representation on boards) as well as enlarging employee-share ownership.

Individualist models

Individualist versions of stakeholding have also continued to attract attention. Tony Blair and Gerhard Schroeder, for example, highlight the importance of stakeholder pensions in their statement on the third way. Given that pensions constitute the largest single item on the social security budget, social security being the largest single item of government expenditure, this means that the area marked for stakeholding is not trivial. Also of importance are proposals originating from centre-left think tanks on assets. In the run-up to the 2001 general election the Fabian Society produced a series of pamphlets relating to ideas for a second-term Labour administration. In one of these pamphlets Julian Le Grand and David Nissan advocate a set of capital grants for all young people (Le Grand and Nissan 2000). Their discussion is couched in terms of welfare policy. Rather than 'curative welfare', which aims to address problems after they arise, they contend their proposal is an example of 'preventative welfare', aiming to address problems before they arise. They draw attention to the unequal distribution of assets within an economy. They note a study by the Institute for Fiscal Studies that estimated that the number of households without assets had risen from 5 per cent 20 years ago, to

10 per cent a decade later. Furthermore the greatest proportion of assetless households, at 20 per cent, are headed by individuals aged 20–24 (Banks and Tanner 1999). Lack of assets matters since it helps perpetuate inequality and prevents individuals from realising opportunities. To tackle this they endorse a £10,000 capital grant to all individuals at age 18. They argue that a substantial sum should be made available to individuals if opportunities are to be substantially enhanced, and consider £10,000 sufficient. Grants would be financed by reform of inheritance tax, and would be universal. This emphasis on universal benefits emanates in part from problems they identify with targeted welfare (namely that targeted welfare is more difficult to administer, more demeaning and more socially divisive than universal welfare), as well as for the reason that the wealth of one generation is a common asset to the next, and so all should have some access to it. The purpose of these grants is to help foster education and accumulation of capital (through investment, for example, in housing or business). They suggest that the grants be paid into an Accumulation of Capital and Education (ACE) account run by trustees who will supervise spending plans. As well as funding education and business start-ups, they suggest it could also be paid into other assets, such as stakeholder pensions.

Le Grand and Nissan note similarities with Ackerman and Alstott's stakeholder proposals, as well as overlaps with proposals coming from the Institute for Public Policy Research. Gavin Kelly and Rachel Lissauer argue that asset-based strategies offer the prospect of a new politics of ownership for the left. Asset-based strategies for these theorists are important since they chime with New Labour's focus on positive welfare (which shifts welfare from income replacement to a scheme that places more weight on human skills and capacities), because empirical evidence suggests that distributing assets has an independent effect on economic outcomes (such as levels of inequality), and this can help steer a continual trend towards greater individualisation in a progressive direction. The points made by Le Grand and Nissan about the current distribution of assets are repeated, and this, Kelly and Lissauer argue, provides a case for reform. They suggest that policies on assets should be governed by a number of principles, namely opportunity, equality, autonomy and responsibility. This resonates with the general focus on real opportunity and responsibility within New Labour. Kelly and Lissauer draw on asset-based policies in the United States when fashioning their own proposals. They note the importance of policies on Individual Development Accounts (IDAs) and Universal Savings Accounts (USAs). Outlining the important role Michael Sherraden played in the emergence of IDAs in the United States, Kelly and Lissauer note that IDAs are savings accounts which 'accumulate funds for specified personal development purposes such as: post-secondary education, training, starting up a business or home ownership' (Kelly and Lissauer 2000, p. 10). Individual contributions to these accounts trigger matching contributions, in varying ratios from state, businesses or non-profit sources. Kelly and Lissauer also highlight USAs announced in President Bill Clinton's 1999 State of the Union Address. Although they note that USAs differ in important ways from the proposals they discuss in a British context, they emphasise that their scale is in contrast to the (as yet) small-scale IDAs in the United States. These accounts use a system of matched savings accounts to provide pensions for those on low incomes or without occupational pension plans. In their proposals, Kelly and Lissauer discuss three main policies. First, IDAs aimed at those on low incomes. They suggest a 3:1 government to individual matched contribution ratio, with funds also possibly given by third parties such as local companies and charities. These accounts would be used for specified investment purposes. They consider using these accounts in conjunction with New Deal schemes, on a local basis or through integration within the social security and/or tax credit systems. The others relate to opportunity funds. Both involve a universal capital endowment, with a means-tested matching savings formula for those on low incomes subject to a maximum figure. Funds would be used for investment purposes such as lifelong learning, training and (first-time) home ownership. A Children's Fund pays a £1000 endowment when a child is born. A Young Adults' Fund would trigger the universal endowment at age 18. The key is that this would promote 'self-improvement, personal responsibility and risk taking' (ibid., p. 21). Asset-based welfare has defined an important research agenda at the IPPR. This agenda is being consolidated and expanded with the formation of the Centre for Asset-Based Welfare. Individuals at these think tanks were also involved in the actual construction of policy. Gavin Kelly, for example, played an important role in drafting proposals for baby-bonds implemented below.

Assessment

A substantial conception of the third way can be identified at a theoretical level, and this overlaps importantly with stakeholder ideas. Collectivist models of stakeholding can be seen in the attention paid to pluralist models of the firm as well as the concept of the public corporation. Individualist models of stakeholding can be detected in the focus on asset-based welfare. Moreover when New Labour first entered government Frank Field was made minister for welfare reform charged to 'think the unthinkable'. Although Field was replaced in this office in July 1998, stakeholder ideas have remained important. His successor Alistair Darling, as seen above, had also expressed sympathy with stakeholder ideas and indeed pressed on with proposals on stakeholder pensions. Further indication of the connection between stakeholding and the third way is given by the fact that some individuals who have used stakeholder discourse have also subsequently used third-way language to refer to a similar set of ideas. This suggests that at least part of third-way theory overlaps with stakeholder ideas. This does not imply that such theorists have simply shifted discourse uncritically. For example Stuart White argues that care has to be taken over use of the term third way since it 'can all too easily be taken to imply that we need, not to modernise, but to exit the social democratic tradition in pursuit of something wholly new and distinctive' (White 1998, p. 18). White in fact has expressed a preference for a return to stakeholder language. Social democrats he argues ought to 'give serious thought to alternatives – including, I think, the less fashionable, but more evocative language of stakeholding' (ibid.). White's use of third-way discourse largely reflects its use by others, rather than originating from any personal commitment to this language.

In assessing discourse it is important to note that the features identified here are not entirely new. The importance of knowledge was an important theme of Anthony Crosland's revisionist social democracy. As such, there is less of a contrast between new and old Labour than proponents of New Labour are prone to suggest at times, and any novelty associated with New Labour is accordingly exaggerated. This does not mean, however, that discourse has not moved onto new ground. Although prior strategies focused on the skills of individuals, of importance here are the institutions through which this is promoted. Instead of top-down mechanisms, an important part of

New Labour discourse has involved examining bottom-up approaches organised around the possession of stakes leading to, for example, the role played by asset-based welfare. This is a new policy sphere for Labour, and consequently points in new directions.

The chapter now turns to an analysis of important features of New Labour's policy approach. In light of the distinction drawn in this book between collectivist and individualist stakeholding, this chapter considers those areas in which collectivist and individualist models have relevance. While the chapter does not provide an exhaustive survey of all policy initiatives that have occurred in these areas, it does look at important themes. The ground covered is sufficient to establish that stakeholding is important for understanding policy. Collectivist stakeholding, as has been seen, is manifested in debates surrounding corporate governance and public services. To examine collectivist approaches it considers New Labour policy towards corporations. To study individualist stakeholding the area of welfare is put under scrutiny. This is because the main thrust of individualist accounts of stakeholding was developed in a welfare context. Given that welfare reform has featured more prominently than the reform of corporations for New Labour, more attention is paid to the examination of welfare policy here.

Corporate governance policy: efficiency and corporate social responsibility

Efficiency

Will Hutton provides some indication that New Labour policy has moved onto some of the terrain supported by theorists of stakeholding when he notes:

> Whisper it softly, but the government's record is much better than it admits in public – another example of New Labour underselling itself for fear of the reaction. As well as the new requirement on pension funds and the proposal to widen directors' responsibilities, the Company Law Review proposes a requirement on companies to disclose and publish a wide range of non-financial information, such as their approach to sustainable development.
> (Hutton 2000b, p. v)

Two themes help frame different policy initiatives: a focus on efficiency and a focus on corporate social responsibility. Efficiency concerns are a central theme of government policy. An important example of this relates to the Company Law Review. Established by the Department for Trade and Industry, this independent examination of the legal framework governing companies is intended to provide the foundations for a white paper. The November 2001 pre-budget report announced a consultation on draft legislation. The Review is significant from a stakeholder perspective since it is an explicit part of its analysis. It notes that the '"stakeholder" issue lay at the heart of the Review, though no consensus on the most appropriate approach' (Company Law Review 1999, p. 3). The Steering Committee contained several contributors to stakeholding models of the firm: John Plender, John Parkinson and John Kay[1]. Efficiency themes are central for the Company Law Review. It claims that its predominant objective is to construct 'policies to facilitate productive and creative activity in the most competitive and efficient way possible' (ibid., p. 8). Although the importance of ethical concerns was accepted, it did not intend 'to make proposals as to how such benefits should be shared or allocated between different participants in the economy, on grounds of fairness, social justice or any similar criteria' (ibid., p. 9). Efficiency issues were considered against the background that

> [asset structures] are changing, and becoming increasingly 'soft', in the sense that a significant portion of the value, or capacity, of a business is to be found in intangibles, rather than tangible assets such as buildings and machinery. Some of these are familiar – the skills of the workforce are particularly (labour now being a resource which requires specific training, development and mutual commitment), other examples are the skills of management in combining workforce, key assets, and often external resources from suppliers of goods and services, into productive teams, and traditional intellectual activities, such as research and development ... [even] businesses with a high fixed and tangible asset component depend on effective deployment of such 'soft' assets.
>
> (Ibid., pp. 13–14)

Knowledge-based competencies are seen as an important part of a firm's asset structure, particularly for the future. Managers have a role in fostering such competencies by constructing productive teams, based on patterns of cooperation. The success of a firm for the Company Law Review is built upon 'effective ongoing relationships with employees, customers, suppliers and others; and the need to maintain the company's business reputation and to consider the impact of its operations on the community and the environment' (Company Law Review 2000, p. 13). Much of the competitive advantage of firms emanates from specific knowledge competencies developed within a firm. Here individuals, through trial and error, engage in a process of mutual learning to work together productively as a team. Each individual learns to play a particular role, which when combined with others, forms a knowledge resource. These knowledge interactions are predicated on cooperation between individuals. Cooperation helps ensure that individuals exchange information and ideas and play their role within a team framework. The creation of knowledge, in a team framework in particular, often requires some prior sharing of information, and cooperation helps ensure that individuals transmit the appropriate information.

To help structure their deliberations, the Review set out two approaches. First, an enlightened shareholder-value approach which 'asserts that this can be achieved within present principles, but ensuring that directors pursue shareholders' interests in an enlightened and inclusive way' (Company Law Review 1999, p. vi). The enlightened shareholder approach sets its analysis within a framework of shareholder priority. However, *enlightened* shareholders ought to take account of others who contribute to a firm's success. Second, a pluralist approach which 'asserts that co-operative and productive relationships will only be optimised when directors are required to balance shareholders' interests with those of others committed to the company' (ibid.). The Review did not set out to choose between these different accounts, looking instead at combining elements of both. This helps underline that its policy recommendations do not reflect only one set of ideas, but instead are made up of different components.

Actual recommendations are thought to imply a fundamental revision of company law for the Review. It argues that the current legal framework satisfies three main purposes. First, companies are formed and managed for shareholders and creditors. Secondly, accounting and disclosure requirements operate for the benefit of (actual and potential) shareholders and creditors, protecting them against breach of contract. Thirdly, public disclosure requirements operate for the benefit of the general community. It was decided however that 'current arrangements lead to directors neglecting the long-term, often under (actual or perceived) misguided pressure from shareholders' (Company Law Review 2000, p. 35). Addressing this implied two broad sets of policy proposals for large companies. The first put forward a statutory set of principles relating to directors' duties obliging them, 'to achieve the success of the company for the benefit of shareholders by taking proper account of all the relevant considerations for that purpose' (ibid., p. 13). The final report noted that this included developing 'positive relationships with a wide range of interests beyond shareholders – such as employees, suppliers and customers' (Company Law Review 2001, p. xi). While asserting the priority of shareholders, it also implies going beyond a narrow focus on shareholder interests. The second set promoted wider accountability. This was to be attained by enhanced reporting requirements for large companies, ensuring that as part of their annual report material would be published which would allow 'users to achieve a proper assessment of the performance and future plans and prospects of the business. It would include, where relevant, its relationships with employees and others and its impact on the community and environment' (Company Law Review 2000, p. 13). In part the provision of this information is intended to promote the exercise of responsible behaviour by shareholders. But it is also intended to emphasise that companies are increasingly reliant on the 'qualitative and intangible assets such as the skills and knowledge of their employees, their business relationships and their reputation. Information about future plans, opportunities, risks and strategies is just as important as the historical review of performance which forms the basis for reporting at present' (Company Law Review 2001, p. 49).

In July 2002 a white paper was published that drew on the Review's recommendations. It agreed with the Review that there should be a statement of managerial duties spelling out the salience of stakeholders. The white paper states that,

> the basic goal for directors should be the success of the company of the collective best interests of shareholders, but that directors should also recognise, as the circumstances require, the company's

> need to foster relationships with its employees, customers and suppliers, its need to maintain its business reputation, and its need to consider the company's impact on the community and the working environment.
>
> (Department of Trade and Industry 2002, p. 26).

The white paper also endorses the Review's conclusion that there should be enhanced reporting requirements of policies adopted towards fostering relationships with employees, customers, suppliers and the wider community. It contends that:

> [a] reporting requirement in these terms would also be a major benefit for a wide cross-section of a company's stakeholders. The new requirement to report, for example, on material environmental issues would be a major contribution to both corporate social responsibility and sustainable development issues. (ibid., p. 38)

Steps to promote efficiency can also be seen in measures taken to improve the quality of institutional investment in the UK. This is seen in the announcement in Budget 2001 that the government would, after consultation, promulgate the principles of the Myners review of institutional investment (Myners 2001). Early in 2000 Paul Myners, chairman of Gartmore Investment Management, was asked to explore and assess institutional investment decisions in the UK. Reporting on 6 March 2001, Myners' report identified significant failings in the nature of institutional investment. In particular, Myners argued that investors often lacked the expertise and incentives to make efficient investment decisions. Alongside a lack of active contact with the companies in which investments were made, there was often a lack of clarity regarding the nature of the investment decisions made. To help rectify this Myners argued for a voluntary code ensuring that decisions were taken only by those with the right skills, backed up by appropriate resources. Objectives should be clearly set out, with regular reporting on investment strategy and returns to members of the investment fund and the public. The report noted that 'the review proposes that annual reporting by all pension funds to their beneficiaries and other interested parties should develop into a forum for decision-makers to explain and justify their approach, and for stakeholders to exercise oversight of the decisions made on their behalf' (ibid., p. 147). Active intervention in companies is also made a duty of managers. Although voluntary, companies would be asked to explain any departures from the code he set out. While Myners concedes that a voluntary code would not satisfy some, he argues it would nevertheless improve the quality of institutional investment.

Corporate social responsibility

Corporate social responsibility has also been an important aspect of policy. Consumer concerns have featured prominently in policy discussions, and in part this focuses on the role of consumers in relation to privatised utilities such as water, gas and electricity. A green paper on this has noted that the regulatory framework needs strengthening to improve accountability and achieve the right balance of interests between consumers and shareholders. It is argued that regulators should have a primary duty to protect the interests of consumers, and all their other obligations should be subject to this. Consumer councils were proposed as a means of communicating consumer concerns. These are representative bodies of consumers that would be set up on an independent statutory basis, and these councils would communicate the interests of local and national consumers to regulators, and disseminate information to consumers (Department of Trade and Industry 1998a). November 2000 saw the establishment of the Gas and Electricity Consumers' Council (also known as energywatch). This body's role covers providing a strong advocacy role for consumers and obtaining and distributing information for consumers on the performance of these utilities.

Moves to institutionalise shareholder concerns can be seen in a consultation on executive pay launched by the Department of Trade and Industry in December 2001. It is noted that although there is currently an acceptable level of transparency of disclosure of individual directors' pay, there is inadequate disclosure of remuneration policy. 'It proposes therefore to require quoted companies to make specific disclosures in respect of key aspects of remuneration policy such as the main parameters and rationale for any share option or other long term incentive scheme' (Department of Trade and Industry 2001, p. 10). It is intended to ensure the 'regulatory framework promotes transparency and accountability to shareholders' (ibid. 2001, p. 5). To foster transparency, companies would be required to publish a report on executive pay as part of the yearly reporting cycle, disclosing details of pay, remuneration policy and the role of remuneration committees in these areas. To promote accountability, the DTI proposes that an annual resolution be put to shareholders on the remuneration report. It is argued that although the vote should be advisory (saying it would not be feasible for shareholders to approve specific levels of pay), 'dialogue between the board and investors on remuneration issues is more likely to be effective if it is underpinned by a requirement for an annual shareholder vote on the remuneration report' (ibid., p. 12).

In October 2001, Secretary of State for Trade and Industry Stephen Byers placed Railtrack (the firm that ran the rail network) into administration. In its place he suggested developing an alternative company in which managers would be responsible to passengers rather than to shareholders. On 27 June 2002 the Secretary of State for Transport Alistair Darling delivered a statement to the House of Commons which declared that a public interest company, Network Rail, had conducted a sale and purchase agreement to acquire Railtrack plc. It will pay £500 million (£300 million of which will be provided by the government). Network Rail will be responsible for operating, maintaining and renewing the rail network. Instead of being accountable to shareholders, directors will be accountable to members of the governing board representing the public interest and the Strategic Rail Authority (the body regulating the railways) (<www.dft.gov.uk>). On 3 October 2002 Network Rail formally completed the acquisition of Railtrack plc (www.networkrail.com <http://www.networkrail.com>).

Welfare policy: responsibility, assets and government protection

Responsibility

The chapter now turns to a study of the contours of welfare policy. Responsibility features heavily in the New Labour emphasis on work. The central motif of New Labour's welfare reform programme is, 'Work for those who can; security for those who cannot' (Department of Social Security 1998a, p. iii). Under New Labour, individuals have an obligation to work if able to do so. This is part of a more general approach emphasising rights and responsibilities, set against two possible alternatives, the first of which is, 'a privatised future with the welfare state becoming a residual safety net for the poorest and most marginalised' (ibid., p. 2). However, for the green paper, an increasingly divided society would be the result, and it would be difficult to generate support from the better off for the welfare bill for the poor. The second alternative is a focus simply on providing 'more generous and costly benefits' (ibid.). Hence the problem for the green paper was essentially twofold. First, this welfare bill would contribute to a rising, and ultimately fiscally unsustainable, welfare bill. Secondly it would provide poor incentives to find work, by contributing to 'benefit traps', where individuals have little incentive to enter work since income out of work may exceed income in work. Part of the focus aims at tackling dependence. Welfare 'should become more focused on helping people to become independent, rather than locking them into dependency' (Department of Social Security 1998b, p. 1). Work is important since it is seen as an active duty that helps inculcate a sense of individual responsibility. To achieve this, there would be, 'a single work-focused gateway into the benefit system for all those who can work, providing customers with a flexible, professional, personalised service. In particular we envisage personal advisers helping claimants develop a tailor-made action plan for regaining their independence' (ibid., p. 81). This appeal to personal responsibility is also supported by a focus on duties towards others, in particular the importance of reciprocity. If the community helps fund an individual's welfare benefits (here unemployment benefit), there is a reciprocal obligation, according to New Labour, to work if so able. A central example of this general approach is the New Deal for the young unemployed. Forming one of the five key pledges in the 1997 general election manifesto, this promised to 'get 250,000 under-25-year-olds off benefit and into work by using money from a windfall levy on the privatised utilities' (Labour Party 1997, p. 40). Four opportunities are offered for unemployed job-seekers under 25 in the green paper. The first is placing the individual in a private sector job using a £60 per week wage subsidy for employers (which would last six months). The second is work with a non-profit-making voluntary organisation, the individual being paid at the benefit rate plus an additional entitlement (lasting for six months). The third is a job with the government's own environmental service taskforce. The fourth is full-time study on an approved course. The green paper notes, 'There is no 'fifth' option of simply remaining on benefit' (Department of Social Security 1998a, p. 25). In fact, 'Those who unreasonably refuse an offer or fail to take up a place will be sanctioned' (ibid., p. 31).

New Deal

The New Deal was funded initially by a one-off 'Windfall Tax' on the privatised utilities. Spending Review 2000 announced that an Employment Opportunities Fund would be established to continue funding of the New Deal once the receipts from the Windfall Tax were spent. Allocating £875 million in 2001–2 and rising to £1.4 billion in 2003–4, this would help establish the New Deal on a permanent basis (HM Treasury 2000a). The New Deal for Young People was launched nationally in April 1998. Since June 2000 the Gateway stage of the programme has been enhanced by providing additional help on soft skills such as presentation, punctuality and communications skills. The November 2001 pre-budget report noted the piloting of greater flexibility of the options section of the New Deal for Young People from that date, to give personal advisers more freedom to tailor support to account for local labour market conditions. A pilot mentoring scheme was also announced to see how monitoring can be used to improve chances of employment, from January 2002 (HM Treasury 2001a).

Budget 2000 announced that a New Deal for those aged over twenty-five would be introduced on a national basis from April 2001. For those unemployed for over eighteen months, there was to be a stronger emphasis on matching rights and responsibilities. This would involve a Gateway lasting up to four months that provided jobsearch advice from a personal adviser. For those aged 25–49 the Gateway would be followed by a compulsory Intensive Activity Period of between 13 and 36 weeks. This would provide support for self-employment, basic employability training, focused and flexible packages of intensive support (for example work placements with employers or voluntary organisations). Access would also be provided to a wage subsidy. At the end of the Intensive Activity Period, individuals would enter a follow-up period lasting three months that would consolidate their skills and experience based on intensive jobsearch. Sanctions applied to the 18–24 age range would also be applied to the 25–49 age range (HM Treasury 2000b). Budget 2002 announced the setting up of mandatory pilot schemes extending eligibility for the New Deal 25+ to all those who have been unemployed for a total of 18 months over the past three years (rather than 18 of the past 21 months) (HM Treasury 2002).

A New Deal for the over-50s that was piloted in October 1999 was rolled out nationally in April 2000. Organised on a voluntary basis, this would be available when an individual (or their partner) had been eligible for benefits for longer than six months. The programme provided a series of options including personal advice, help with job-search, an employment credit of £60 per week for full-time work or £40 per week for part-time or self-employment, or in-work training support.

The New Deal for Lone Parents was launched nationally in October 1998 and targeted at those on Income Support. This involved job-search help from a personal adviser. From autumn 2001, this advice would be made available to all lone parents not working, or working less than 16 hours per week. From April 2001, lone parents with children would be required to meet an adviser. A set of voluntary options would be provided including the opportunity to undertake education and training with a £15 a week premium on top of Income Support from April 2001, allowing individuals to work under 16 hours a week with a £20 per week disregard and a childcare tax credit. The November 2001 pre-budget report noted that from November 2001 eligibility for the New Deal for Lone Parents would be extended to all lone parents who were not working, or working less than 16 hours a week.

Emphasis is placed upon involving institutions other than the state in the delivery of the welfare reform programme. Focus is placed upon involving employers, non-profit-making voluntary organisations and training institutions in the four options a job-seeker faces. In fact employers have played a particularly important role in the delivery of the New Deal, with the government keen to encourage businesses to advertise and provide the New Deal. The November 2001 pre-budget report notes that employer involvement is core to the success of the New Deal programmes. To encourage partnerships with local employers, Local Account Managers would be created in all Jobcentre Plus Offices with national roll-out intended from April 2002. Jobcentre Plus was launched in October 2001 (in 49 pathfinder areas across the country) bringing together the Employment Service and those parts of the Benefit Agency dealing with working-age individuals to provide an integrated service to help people get back to work. Budget 2002 noted that Jobcentre Plus was already operational in 56 offices and that a further 225 new offices would be established between October 2002 and April 2003. The November 2001 pre-budget report also noted the formation of Action Teams in 53 areas of England, Scotland and Wales. Government would work in partnership with employers and voluntary organisations to help devise strategies to reduce unemployment.

Work and security

The stress on work is also extended to those who have typically been a focus for security. Certain groups of individuals have traditionally been the focus of security within welfare policy, and comprise those who fall outside of the circle of adults capable of participating fully in employment. Working-age adults in employment are not generally thought to be in need of assistance to meet their personal needs. Departures from each of the following characteristics are thought to imply a focus on security. This points to three broad groups of people. First, those people who are not adults, that is, children. Second, those persons who are not fully able, that is, people with disabilities. Lastly, those individuals who are no longer eligible for employment, that is, pensioners. Emphasis is placed, however, on getting as many individuals to work as possible under New Labour. This has been extended to some of those traditionally offered security. Most obviously this relates to disabled individuals. With regard to the disabled, those 'who could work are too often consigned to a life on benefits' (Department of Social Security 1998c, p. 1). Receipt of Incapacity Benefit is dependent on the results of an All Work Test. The test focuses exclusively on what individuals cannot do. It is argued however that this 'sends the wrong messages to people who are trying to make the most of their potential' (ibid., p. 4). The All Work Test would be reformed, with greater emphasis on a gateway approach to 'strengthen the link between work and entitlement' (Department of Social Security 1998d, p. 6). To promote the transition of disabled individuals into work, a Disabled Person's Tax Credit (DPTC) was introduced in October 1999. This would be offered to those people with disabilities who work for more than 16 hours per week. For a full-time worker with a family and children, this would help provide a minimum income of £246 per week (HM Treasury 2000a).

The November 2001 pre-budget report noted that from April 2002 people on Incapacity Benefit would allow claimants to undertake up to 16 hours of work a week for 12 months (earning up to £66 a week) without any loss in benefit. Budget 2002 notes that from April 2002 the DPTC with the minimum wage guarantees a minimum weekly income of £172 for an individual in full-time work (and with the Working Tax Credit mentioned below, the minimum weekly income is £194).

The focus on work is also seen in proposals aimed at the young. For New Labour, having a parent in work provides an active role model to children. To support the transition into work, a Working Families Tax Credit (WFTC) was launched in October 1999. In conjunction with the minimum wage, the WFTC guarantees a minimum income of £214 per week for a family with children and with someone in full-time work (HM Treasury 2000b). In addition to making work pay, attention is paid to childcare since for many families, 'the cost of childcare is a major obstacle to work' (Department of Social Security 1998a, p. 58). A £470 million National Childcare Strategy was launched in 1998 aimed at improving the accessibility, quality and affordability of childcare. A childcare component of the WFTC provides up to 70 per cent of eligible childcare costs, to a limit of £100 per week for a family with one child, and £150 per week for two or more children (HM Treasury 2000b). The November 2001 pre-budget report noted that these figures were increased from June 2001 to £135 and £200 per week respectively. The November 2000 pre-budget report announced plans for a single tax credit from 2003 integrating different strands for children emanating from WFTC, DPTC and Income Support (HM Treasury 2000c). The November 2001 pre-budget report noted that this new Working Tax Credit would also be extended to encompass those without children. This would be complemented by a new Child Tax Credit. Budget 2002 stated that the Working Tax Credit would be available from April 2004. It would guarantee a minimum income of £183 a week for a single earner couple without children, aged 25 and over and working full-time on the minimum wage. A family with one child and one full-time worker on the minimum wage would be guaranteed an income of £237 per week. It also noted that from April 2003 eligibility for the childcare tax credit element of the Working Tax Credit would include those who used approved childcare at their own home. As well as easing the transition into work, New Labour has pursued policies to support parents once in work. Budget 2001, for example, extended maternity cover from 18 to 26 weeks and increased maternity pay from £60.20 to £100 per week as well as introducing two weeks paid paternity leave.

Assets and opportunity

Attention to assets is a prominent theme of policy. Asset-based policies are seen in a framework of promoting real opportunity and responsibility. The government insists that in order for individuals to maintain employment in the global economy, they must continually engage in the updating of skills. This means attention to acquiring skills throughout their life. This concerns leads to the two

> initiatives which exemplify our approach: individual learning accounts which enable men and women to take responsibility for their own learning with support from both Government and employers; and the University for Industry which will offer access to a learning network to help people deepen their knowledge, update their skills and gain new ones.
>
> (Department for Education and Employment 1998, p. 8)

Individual learning accounts (ILAs) 'will be used, at the learner's choice, to pay for learning – whether an evening class, or a learning programme through the UFI, or meeting the cost of childcare so as to give time to study' (ibid., p. 27). It notes, 'Learning accounts will be built on two key principles: first, that individuals are best placed to choose what and how they want to learn; and second, that responsibility for investing in learning is shared' (ibid.). These accounts for New Labour were based on the proposition, first, that individuals are best able to identify their particular human capital needs, and secondly that they also have a responsibility to invest in their human capital development. The paper sought to test out a variety of different approaches in preparation for a national system. An important theme in the above accounts of stakeholding is the idea of distributing stakes as widely as possible. One aspect of policy has been greater attention paid to issues of coverage among a population, that is whether stakes should be universal or targeted at particular sections of a given population. This is seen in the discussion of ILAs.

The paper proposed to set up initially one million learning accounts, funded by £150 million from Training and Enterprise Council (TEC) resources. It considered two possible systems, 'the *universal* approach will offer accounts to anyone at work wanting to learn. Everyone will have to invest a minimum amount of his or her own money in their account, either as a lump sum or in the form of a commitment to regular saving. The government will then support that initial investment, up to a maximum public contribution of £150 for each account. It will then be open to others – for example, employers – to contribute to a person's account in cash or in kind' (ibid., p. 28). The alternative '*targeted* approach will use a proportion of these one million accounts to support particular learning or skill needs; for example, people without qualifications and in low-skill jobs, areas of skill shortages, employees in small firms, and those seeking to return to work' (ibid.). The UFI is to act as a national coordinating institution that individuals may contact to enquire about their specific training needs. A variety of methods may be used to contact the UFI, from e-mail, letter, fax or telephone, to visiting local UFI sites based at supermarkets, high-street shops and colleges. Courses may take a variety of different formats: television broadcasts, a CD-ROM or evening classes. Evening classes would be delivered through local institutions such as libraries, further education colleges and firms. The UFI would be responsible for stimulating, as well as satisfying, demand for training through an appropriate marketing and advertising campaign. Various target areas would be prioritised according to the report, including information technology and management skills. Government intervention, through a public–private partnership, would be used to fund the UFI.

ILAs were implemented nationally in 2000. Available to all individuals aged 19 or over, special emphasis was placed on promoting these accounts among those aged between 19 and 30, those returning to employment, the self-employed and non-teaching school staff. To encourage take-up, the first million account holders to book training would receive special benefits (for example, by providing £150 as long as individuals contributed £25). The Economic and Fiscal Strategy Report 2000 noted that people in England would be given an 80 per cent discount on computer literacy courses, and a fifth off the costs of other selected activities (Northern Ireland and Scotland set their own priorities). A target of one million accounts was set for March 2002. Budget 99 announced that workers who hold

ILAs would pay no tax on national insurance contributions on their employer contribution towards their learning (provided that employers made help available for all employees). The November 2000 pre-budget report announced that from autumn 2000 learndirect (the brand name for the UFI) was rolling out its information communications technology learning portal nationally. 700 learndirect centres were established around the country, with 600 new centres announced in September 2000 (HM Treasury 2000c).

The scheme appeared to be popular since it provoked considerable demand. In November 2001, however, the newly installed Secretary of State for Education and Skills, Estelle Morris, announced that ILAs were to be suspended. There is some controversy surrounding the reasons for this decision. The official government line seemed to suggest that ILAs were suspended because of concerns over fraud. In particular, there were worries about the quality of training provided by supplier organisations. A prime concern was that bodies with little experience in providing training were being set up and signing people up for courses. After people paid for courses they found they were provided with sub-standard material. Such organisations saw ILAs as an opportunity simply to make money (Bennett and Kelly 2001). The House of Commons education select committee raised doubts about this explanation, however, during an interrogation of the adult skills minister John Healey on 28 November 2001. It was suggested instead that the government had not properly budgeted for the success of the initiative and were taken aback by its popularity. The programme had to be stopped to prevent it being overwhelmed by demand (Crequer 2001). Neither of the problems identified in the different explanations about the withdrawal of ILAs appears insurmountable. One way of tackling the possibility of supplier fraud is to insist that only those bodies that pass a quality assurance test (and are given a 'kitemark') are entitled to provide training. If ILAs have to fall broadly within the original budget, greater restrictions can be imposed on those who are able to claim such accounts. Whichever version of events one believes, the potential remains for developing a more robust form of this measure. The new adult skills minister Ivan Lewis announced in June 2002 that proposals were being made for a new form of ILA that imposed more stringent checks on learning providers (though it was also admitted that there was an overspend of £93.6 million on the original version over 2001) (Hook 2002).

To help generate the commitment of workers to firms, attention is paid to the use of employee share-options. A consultation process on the use of employee share-ownership schemes was announced in the Treasury's November 1998 pre-budget report, and support for such schemes was announced in the 1999 Budget to 'encourage workers to take a stake in the success of their companies' (HM Treasury 1999, p. 3). Greater 'financial participation – through employee share-ownership or stock options – is already a tool applied in some knowledge driven industries (e.g. computing), and is likely to become more widespread' (Department of Trade and Industry 1998b, p. 19). Finance Act 2000 introduced an All-Employee Share Ownership Plan (AESOP). To encourage shareholding this Act applied the more generous business assets rate of capital gains tax taper relief to all disposals of shares held by employees. The November 2000 pre-budget report set a target of 500,000 more employee shareholders by 2005, bringing the total to 2.5 million. By March 2001, 282 applications from workplaces had been received and over 100,000 employees were covered by the plan. To improve the plan, Budget 2001 announced a stamp duty exemption introduced for employees buying shares through an AESOP trust (HM Treasury 2001b).

The November 2001 pre-budget report noted that the government was testing the creation of Employment Zones to help tackle unemployment for those individuals aged 25 or over. Here jobseekers and their advisers would be able to set up Personal Job Accounts to make flexible use of funds available to help overcome barriers to work.

Assets and responsibility

Proposals on responsibility can be seen in attempts to encourage individuals to save for their own future. The 1998 pensions green paper proposed that stakeholder pensions would be targeted at those who have not usually found it worthwhile to take on a personal pension if not covered by an occupational pension. Stakeholder pensions were originally targeted at those earning between £9000 and £18,500 per year. The paper accepts that there may be a transitional stage before stakeholder pensions are fully operable, and while such pensions are being established moderate earners are likely to remain with the Second State Pension. The State Second Pension is a replacement for the State Earnings Related Pension Scheme

(SERPS). SERPS is a pay-as-you-go scheme provided by the state for those who earn enough National Insurance contributions and who are not contracted out into an occupational or private pension. Within the Second State Pension the value of SERPS would be doubled on contributions up to £9000 per year, and those who earned less than £9000 per year would be treated as if they had earned £9000 per year when their pension is calculated. However, once the stakeholder pensions are fully functioning, individuals will have incentives to contract out and take stakeholder pensions. Those who earn above £18,500 per year are thought by the paper to possess already a second pension scheme, either occupational or private. Such schemes are, and will generally be, preferable, for the paper, to the proposals for a State Second Pension and stakeholder pensions. Indeed this is the preference of the paper: it does not aim to substitute, but to complement private or occupational provision (Department of Social Security 1998d). These pensions were made available from April 2001. The November 2001 pre-budget report noted that from 8 October 2001 employers without pension schemes who employ five or more staff are required to offer stakeholder pensions. Those without earnings are also able to contribute at least £3600 a year to a stakeholder pension, ensuring that those on a career break or bringing up children can contribute to such a pension. Individuals earning less than £30,000 a year are also able to contribute to a stakeholder pension alongside an occupational scheme.

Budget 2001 noted the introduction of a Pensions Credit from 2003. This is intended to reward those who have built up savings during their working lives, or are working beyond retirement age. Under the current system, pensioners on the minimum income guarantee lose a pound of benefit for every extra pound of their second pension or earnings income. In its place, individuals will be rewarded for saving with a pensioner's post-credit income, which will be at least 60p above the guaranteed minimum income level for every pound of second pension, savings or earnings income they build above the basic state pension (HM Treasury 2001b).

Policy has also focused on other instruments to promote saving. In 1999 individual savings accounts were introduced. Replacing tax-exempt special savings accounts and personal equity plans, individual savings accounts were opened by 8.5 million people in their first year (HM Treasury 2001b). Budget 2001 announced the implementation of individual pension accounts from April 2001. These accounts offer a way of holding assets inside a pension scheme. Proposals were also implemented to exempt collective investment from stamp duty reserve tax where the assets involved are within individual pension accounts. Drawing from the United States, attention was also paid to the setting up of individual development accounts that would entail government providing matching funds for savers. To promote flexibility attention was also paid to integrating these different schemes. Budget 2000 underlined that money in an individual savings account can be transferred into stakeholder pensions, and that savings built up in a tax-free employee share scheme can be transferred to either an individual savings account or a stakeholder pension while remaining in a tax-free environment.

Responsibility has also led to a focus on capital grant schemes. Budget 2001 announced that from April 2001 a children's tax credit would be established (paid for from money gained from abolishing the married couples' allowance) worth £10 per week (this credit was also reflected in higher Income Support and Jobseeker's Allowance credits). From April 2002, £20 per week would be made available in the year of a child's birth, making this a £1000 'baby bonus' (ibid.). The November 2001 pre-budget report also highlighted a consultation on the implementation of proposals on a Child Trust Fund. This is a proposal for a universal account, with endowments paid at birth, and at ages 5, 11 and 16. Children from the poorest families will receive most help. Parents, friends, families and children will be able to contribute to these accounts. It is noted that the consultation is considering two models. One is an 'open-market' model where the Child Trust Fund will be administered by financial service providers. The second is a 'preferred panel' model with a more limited number of providers offering the Child Trust Fund in partnership with government. Budget 2002 stated that it expects to update its proposals in the run-up to Budget 2003. The November 2001 pre-budget report also noted a consultation on a Savings Gateway. Targeted at low-income individuals, these are accounts containing government-funded matches for all money saved up to a limit. Budget 2002 announced a pilot programme for the Savings Gateway from August 2002, lasting two and a half years (including evaluation). It is perhaps worth noting, however, that in relation to moves to implement capital grant schemes, this is an area in which action has lagged behind rhetoric. In particular, although government has made a number of prominent declarations on such measures, in practice it has moved slowly to implement this. Although it is likely that some version of these initiatives will emerge, this is not (as with other features at a consultative stage) completely certain. Care, accordingly, has to be exercised when looking at the government's record. The administration displays a tendency to exaggerate its own achievements (including those that overlap with stakeholder ideas). This is not to say that no truth is contained in New Labour announcements, only that they are not as far-reaching as is sometimes suggested.

Government help

Although much of the above focuses on individuals meeting their own welfare needs, an important part of policy accepts that government has to take action in particular situations to protect individuals. This relates to those who can and those who cannot work. Part of the focus on paid work is driven by an attack on poverty. Paid work is seen, in particular, as necessary for tackling poverty, although it is accepted that paid work is not always sufficient to prevent poverty. For example, certain individuals may belong to the 'working poor'. Here individuals may not earn enough in jobs to lift them out of poverty. Tackling this has led to one important strand in New Labour policy, namely a project of 'making work pay'. This has involved the institution of a national minimum wage, which was introduced in April 1999. For workers aged 22 and over, this was initially set at £3.60 per hour, with Budget 2001 announcing a rise to £4.10 per hour from October 2001, and £4.20 per hour from October 2002. For trainees the minimum wage was set at £3.20 per hour and £3 per hour for those aged between 18 and 21, and Budget 2002 announced that this rate would be increased to £3.60 per hour from October 2002. Funding the minimum wage has meant some redistribution through the tax system.

Redistribution is also seen for those who cannot work. Not all individuals can be pressed into work. For those who cannot, New Labour places emphasis on government protection. In relation to children a Sure Start programme was established to help tackle social exclusion among pre-school children. By 2003–4 this would have resources worth £500 million. Sure Start programmes are managed by local partnerships of parents, voluntary groups, private organisations and statutory services. The November 2001 pre-budget report noted that 430 programmes had already been announced (with 200 operational). By March 2004, 500 programmes would cover one third of those children in poverty. In 1998 the Department for Social Security announced: 'Child Benefit should and will remain universal where it is already universal and should be paid as now, directly to the mother, with an increase in the rate of benefit for the oldest child of £2.50 a week from April next year. Families throughout the country – including those on means-tested benefits – will gain from this investment. It must be right in principle that if child benefit is raised in future, then there is a case for higher rate tax payers paying tax on it' (Department of Social Security 1998a, p. 58). The November 2001 pre-budget report noted that over the first parliament Child Benefit had increased in real terms by 26 per cent for the first child. It is worth £15.50 a week for the first child and £10.35 a week for subsequent children.

Redistribution is used for people with disabilities. For example, in 1998 a new Disability Income Guarantee for the poorest was announced, ensuring that single people receive at least £128 per week, and couples £169 a week. From April 2001, these figures rose to £142 a week for single people, £186.80 for couples (HM Treasury 2001). Particular emphasis is given to helping those disabled early in life, which is before age 20. These individuals qualify for Severe Disability Allowance. However 70 per cent of these individuals have to rely on means-tested Income Support to supplement their income needs. To help alleviate this, the Severe Disability Allowance would be reformed to provide more help for those disabled early in life. After a year on benefit, these individuals would be entitled to £78.30 a week as compared with £52.70 per week.

Redistribution is also seen in proposals towards the retired. To help the poorest pensioners, emphasis was placed upon securing a minimum income guarantee. From April 1999 this would be at least £75 per week for single pensioners, and £116.60 per week for couples. Budget 2001 announced an increase to £92.15 a week for single pensioners and £140.55 a week for couples. The minimum income guarantee is delivered through the basic state pension, and Income Support. Budget 2001 increased the basic state pension by £5 to £72.50 a week in April 2001, and a further £3 a week from April 2002 for single pensioners. Couples enjoyed an increase of £8 to £115.90 a week from April 2001, and a further £4.80 a week from April 2002. From 1997 to 2001 this meant the average pensioner household was £11 a week better off, with most pensioner households better off if there was an earnings link in the basic state pension. Budget 2002 noted that in 2003–4 there would be a guaranteed minimum income for single pensioners and couples of £100 and £160 per week respectively. To help provide general security, winter fuel payments were introduced in 1997. Paid to every household containing someone 60 or over, by December 2000 this amounted to £200. Free television licences were provided to the over-75s from November 2000 (HM Treasury 2001).

Policy assessment

The analysis of New Labour policy suggests that there exist several distinct, and partially overlapping, agendas. This is perhaps clearest in relation to welfare policy. Within this context, for example, elements of Keynesian social democracy can be detected. This is seen most clearly perhaps in the continuing importance of state spending for policies such as Child Benefit. The focus on paid work reflects in part a conventional social democratic concern with alleviating poverty. Paid work is seen as the central way in which poverty may be alleviated. For New Labour, this has involved elements of a traditional social democratic concern with redistribution. Such commitments have played an increasingly prominent role in policy, inspired in part perhaps by the importance attached to satisfying the preferences of core Labour voters.

The existence of a significant Conservative agenda can also be detected. Advocates of free markets tend to focus on provision of residual welfare. Here individuals make their own welfare provision privately through the market, with public policy intervention occurring only for those unable to provide adequately for their own future. Emphasis is placed on implementing targeted or selective welfare, and this is often manifested with a focus on means tests. Individuals including Frank Field have criticised New Labour for having elements of selective welfare. He notes,

> Part of thinking the unthinkable was to accept that welfare affects behaviour and thereby the character of recipients. Means test are

> powerful teaching agents against working, saving and being honest. Implicit in Labour's approach before the election was a disengagement from means tests ... So far the government has set sail in the opposite direction.
>
> (Field 1998, p. 8)

Whereas Field wants to rely only on a new universal system, New Labour policy has elements of selective welfare. This helps structure proposals on, for example, stakeholder pensions. Whereas Field advocated compulsory pensions for all, eventual proposals are voluntary and targeted at a particular income group. This is not to say that proposals for stakeholder pensions did not break new ground, rather that they are interwoven with free-market assumptions. Field suggests that this focus on free-market principles will wreck the government's steps on stakeholder pensions. In particular, the minimum income guarantee for pensioners will undermine the incentives of those in the target group for stakeholder pensions to take out such pensions (Field 2000).

The above analysis implies that New Labour's policy record is not all of a piece. Different agendas can be detected. Moreover at times these agendas overlap, adding further complexities to policy. Existing proposals for stakeholder pensions, for example, combine elements of a stakeholder approach with a free-market focus on targeting. An implication of this understanding is that those accounts that rely on blanket characterisations of New Labour policy are likely to be unsatisfactory. Although a Conservative agenda can be detected in New Labour policy, seeing policy simply in terms of catch-up to free markets obscures the importance of other agendas. Similarly, those accounts of policy that accept that New Labour departs from free markets but deny the existence of social democratic credentials ignore the existence of a Keynesian social democratic agenda.

The above, however, points to the continuation of older agendas rather than the institution of a new agenda. A new policy agenda can nevertheless be detected. An important part of this overlaps with stakeholding. Box 6.1 contains a summary of some of these developments. One strand intersects with collectivist approaches. This is seen, for instance, in proposals towards companies. There are signs of attempts to engage with and incorporate stakeholder claims in the governance of firms, as is seen in areas such as the Company Law Review. Given the salience of company law for the structure, conduct

Box 6.1 Examples of stakeholder initiatives

Individualist stakeholding	*Collectivist stakeholding*
Real Opportunity • Individual Learning Accounts • Employee share-ownership	*Efficiency* • Company Law Review • Myners' Review
Responsibility • New Deals (for young people, over 25s, over 50s and lone parents) • Stakeholder pensions • Capital grants ('baby bonds', Child Trust Fund, Savings Gateway)	*Responsibility* • Gas and Electricity Consumer Council • Shareholder voting on executive pay • Network rail

and performance of firms, the attention paid to the claims of stakeholders is not trivial. Individualist strands are seen in the moves made to implement asset-based welfare, and this area is being consolidated. The 2001 Manifesto notes that the 'active welfare state has so far been based on work, finance, and services. It is now time to add a fourth pillar to the welfare state – a programme to extend to all children the advantages that come from reaching adulthood backed by a financial nest-egg' (Labour Party 2001, p. 27). In addition to the above, there is also an examination of how these ideas may be applied to other policy areas. For example, in housing policy, a commitment is made to 'examine ways in which tenants can be helped to gain an equity stake in the value of their home' (ibid., p. 14). This is not to deny that policy action has often been less far-reaching than rhetoric. For example the sums devoted to proposals on capital grants are less than those advocated by individuals such as Gavin Kelly and Rachel Lissauer. This, in part, is to be expected. Even if ideas straightforwardly determine policy (although, as noted above, this is not usually the case), there is likely to be a lag between the articulation of policy and its implementation. Notwithstanding this, New Labour action can be seen as more cautious than its rhetoric. This does not mean, however, that it has not moved in new directions. Insofar as New Labour is associated with such an agenda, there is substance to New Labour, and it is not merely spin.

Conclusion

The ground covered in this chapter is offered in support of the second main claim of this book, namely that stakeholding remains important for New Labour. As noted in the introductory chapter, when stakeholding first emerged it attracted the interest of leading New Labour figures such as Tony Blair. It seemed set to define New Labour's project in government. Despite this auspicious start its impact appeared to evaporate in the face of sustained attacks from Conservative commentators. A commonplace view is that stakeholding ultimately had little influence on the evolution of New Labour. This chapter has contested this, arguing that stakeholding is still important for understanding New Labour ideology and policy. It is not the case that we are merely witnessing the long-drawn-out death of stakeholding. This is because New Labour is currently developing and consolidating stakeholder reforms. More specifically, both ideology and policy share overlap with collectivist and individualist strands of stakeholding. While New Labour has arguably shown more interest in individualist strains of stakeholding, the impact of collectivist accounts cannot be ignored. Furthermore, given that the book has contended that stakeholding furnishes a third-way alternative to free markets and Keynesian social democracy, there is some justice in the claim that New Labour is charting a third way. While analysis must accept the continuing significance of free markets and Keynesian social democracy for understanding New Labour, the concept of a third way must not be dismissed. Stakeholding is an important element of this, whatever else it may contain. Having now covered the theoretical and practical aspects of stakeholding the book finishes with a summary and set of brief reflections.

7
Conclusion

In 1992 Labour suffered a fourth successive general election defeat to the Conservative party. The centre-left was at a low ebb. It had been dominated electorally, and the ideas that had formed its main policy outlook from 1945 to the mid-1970s seemed broken and exhausted. If the centre-left was to remain relevant, it had to renew itself. Although this process began in the late 1980s, the renewal was still incomplete by the early 1990s. Stakeholding was important, since it stepped into this breach. It seemed to offer a 'third way' between policies previously adopted by Labour and the Conservatives. This book has argued that the set of stakeholder ideas that emerged furnishes a coherent set of principles to inform public policy that are viable in modern conditions and are distinct from Keynesian social democracy and free markets. Furthermore, although New Labour has backtracked from its initial position on stakeholding, this remains important for comprehending ideology and policy.

To demonstrate this the book embarked on a study of two important branches of stakeholder theory. Collectivist stakeholding was the subject of Chapter 2. These models develop stakeholder approaches within the context of collectivist institutions. One important part of this is rooted in discussions about the governance of business. Beginning with an analysis of Will Hutton's ideas, Chapter 2 argued that the most robust models of corporate governance were developed by thinkers such as John Kay and John Plender. It argued that individual responsibility and knowledge organised around the possession of stakes is at the centre of their view of stakeholder corporations. The chapter then went on to examine how the principles underpinning corporate governance were applied more generally. This looked, specifically, at the public realm. The intellectual foundations of this as articulated by writers such as David Marquand, were set out, as were policy prescriptions.

Chapter 3 considered accounts of 'individualist stakeholding'. This branch emphasises the importance of the individual possession of stakes. It explored how such models emerge in accounts within the economy and welfare. With respect to the economy it was noted that this kind of stakeholding is seen in the criticisms of corporate governance stakeholding by such writers as David Soskice, Charles Leadbeater and Geoff Mulgan. In relation to welfare, the chapter looked at an early manifestation of this in modern British politics, examining the Conservative attempt to create a popular capitalism during the 1980s. This illustrated that stakeholding is not the exclusive property of any political tradition. Nevertheless, the most developed current version, and the one that is most interesting, appears on the centre-left, especially in relation to social democracy. The chapter looked at how these ideas were translated into policies such as stakeholder pensions. Although a variety of justifications may be given for the distribution of stakes, it was contended that these different accounts concentrated on supporting the acquisition of responsibility and knowledge organised around the possession of stakes.

Chapter 4 examined the institutional and ownership context associated with stakeholding. At an institutional level it was argued that stakeholding places weight on a bottom-up context organised around a mix of civil society and markets. It was contended that collectivist and individualist accounts give more emphasis to civil society and markets respectively. As civil society and markets may be constructed in a variety of ways, the nature of these in collectivist and individualist accounts was examined. The ownership agenda was also scrutinised, with particular attention drawn to a hybrid agenda that stressed examining the different combinations of the rights and responsibilities of property, as well as a plural agenda that looked at how property is distributed. It was argued that both agendas are important in stakeholding, although collectivist and individualist accounts give priority to hybridity and plurality respectively.

Chapter 5 argued that stakeholding is robust against charges of incoherence, it constitutes a set of principles that differ from free markets and Keynesian social democracy, and that stakeholding is viable in the global economy. Differences with other components within third-way space were set out to highlight the distinctiveness of the stakeholder position. The chapter then set out the ways in which these different versions of stakeholding overlapped, and the tensions that arose from this.

Chapter 6 explored stakeholding within the context of New Labour, arguing that stakeholding is an important element of New Labour thought and policy. That is not to say that New Labour thinking and policy can only be seen in these terms, rather that stakeholding overlaps importantly with both of these domains for New Labour.

Third way

The two central claims made in this book, namely that stakeholding furnishes the centre-left with a feasible set of third-way principles and that it remains important for understanding New Labour thought and policy carry a number of implications. One of the most important concerns the ways in which the third way and New Labour are viewed. The notion of the third way has attracted much attention in British politics in recent times. One temptation is to treat the third way as a mere slogan. On this view, while supporters of the third way can say what they are against, they cannot give a positive account of what they stand for. This book suggests that this position is mistaken. It is true that a good deal of the rhetoric surrounding the third way is self-serving. There is an element, for instance, of caricature in how Keynesian social democracy and free markets are characterised. The benefits that the third way are said to yield are often exaggerated. Moreover the term 'third way' is not entirely satisfactory. The space mapped out between Keynesian social democracy and free markets is large and compatible with a range of projects. *The* third way masks the possibility of a *variety* of third ways. In spite of these (and other) caveats, it is important from the perspective of this book not to dismiss the notion of the third way out of hand. The concept of stakeholding does provide the centre-left with a viable account of third-way principles to reform public policy. This means that rather than seeing the third way as empty, serious attention ought to be paid to examining its assumptions and implications. None of this is to suppose the superiority or otherwise of third-way reforms over Keynesian social democracy or free markets. It is possible to accept that the third way is not vacuous while also advocating a public policy agenda built mainly around free markets or Keynesian social democracy. In deciding such issues, however, it is important to study the whole range of alternatives that are available, including the third way. There are reasons to suggest, however, that most agendas for public policy will find it useful to draw, at least in part, on some of the themes raised by the third way. For example, the third way is likely to play some role in fostering economic efficiency. The notion of market failure means, by definition, that there are certain areas of public policy in which recourse cannot be made to the use of market mechanisms. Insofar as these realms are still the object for policy, reliance has to be made on intervention by public institutions. This may have to depend, in part, on the state. However, it is unlikely that efficiency will be promoted only by using the state. The sort of critiques of state intervention by supporters of free markets (as outlined in Chapter 1) have some force that needs to be acknowledged. In such circumstances, it is advantageous to use non-state mechanisms. This points to the importance of third-way reforms. It may be that use of the third way is only considered suitable for areas such as these, and in a wider arena use should be made of other mechanisms. However, even conceived in this manner the third way has a salient role in public policy (which expands, the wider the role it adopts). Noting that the third way has substance, therefore, is of value when constructing and implementing public policy initiatives.

As stated above, and as noted in Chapter 5, it is important, however, to separate out different strands of the third way. Stakeholding constitutes only one component in third way space. However there are reasons to suggest that stakeholding is likely to play a salient role in any overall package of third way reforms. Part of this emanates from the fact that stakeholding has valuable contributions to make to a number of areas. For example, one of its strengths is that it directly confronts issues concerned with the governance of corporations. Firms are one of the key institutions in a capitalist economy. In spite of their importance, less attention has often been paid to analysing the governance of firms than to other institutions such as parliament, the judiciary and the executive. This comparative neglect needs to be addressed if the centre-left is to mould an effective reform agenda. The fact that stakeholding directly confronts such issues means that it is likely to be salient in any examination of firms. This does not mean that all have to agree with the answers that stakeholding provides. However, the sorts of questions and issues raised by stakeholding are probably important for any centre-left analysis of firms. Similar things can be said about the contribution that stakeholding makes to the discussion of the reform of public services, or the appropriate rights and responsibilities of ownership. Stakeholding is also likely to be important for any centre-left reform agenda because of its potential popularity. A policy of distributing ownership stakes is one agenda that will probably capture the imagination of the public. Policies for the reform of corporations are also likely to resonate with widespread concerns over corporate performance. For these and other considerations there is good reason to suggest that any centre-left agenda will draw, at least in part, on themes raised by stakeholding.

One question that may be asked is whether stakeholding can be thought of as a political philosophy. A coherent set of ideas need not be thought of as a political philosophy (Keynesian social democracy is usually thought to provide a coherent set of principles for reforming public policy, but it is not typically regarded as a political philosophy). It has been noted in this book that different sides to stakeholding can be identified. The existence of this diversity makes it possible to imagine situations in which stakeholding is compatible with a range of distributive goals. This yields more or less egalitarian versions of stakeholding. As such it might be said that stakeholding ought not to be seen as a political philosophy, but rather a set of ideas that cuts across political philosophies proper. Against this it may be contended that the fact that more or less egalitarian versions of stakeholding can be fashioned should not in itself preclude it being viewed as a political philosophy. Liberalism, for example, is commonly taken to be one of the main political philosophies in Britain. It is possible to mould liberalism, however, so that it serves different distributive ends. Accounts of 'negative liberty' that dedicate resources to ensuring that individuals are free from constraint have different distributive implications than versions of 'positive liberty' that stress providing people with resources so that they acquire certain capabilities. The existence of this variety is usually not thought, in itself, to disqualify liberalism from being considered a political philosophy. Similarly, the fact that stakeholding can be fashioned to meet different distributive ends should not mean, on its own, that it should not be thought of as a political philosophy. Ruling out features that are not important for a political philosophy is not the same, however, as setting out what it is that establishes a political philosophy. Setting out what defines a political philosophy is a large topic beyond the scope of this particular book. It is not strictly necessary to address this to support one of the main claims of the book, namely that stakeholding furnishes a coherent set of principles to animate reforms of public policy. This remains the case whether one believes that stakeholding is best seen as a political philosophy or rather, like Keynesian social democracy, as an organising framework for public policy.

New Labour

The claim that stakeholding is important for understanding New Labour thinking and policy also has a number of implications. It underlines, for example, that stakeholding has relevance at a practical policy level. This supports the contention of this book that stakeholding represents a policy agenda that is viable in current circumstances. This enhances the significance of stakeholding. It means that stakeholding extends beyond the level of discussion and has real consequences for economic and social policy. Its significance at a theoretical level is embellished by its contribution to policy (which is arguably the ultimate aim of any perspective in public policy). The book also has consequences for how New Labour is seen and treated. As with the third way, there have been many debates about the character of New Labour. One standpoint is to treat New Labour with derision, that is, as spin and no substance. The book suggests that such a stance would be flawed. While the rhetoric hovering around New Labour suffers from the same tendency demonstrated in debates over the third way to be self-serving, it is wrong to dismiss it as constituting nothing different in British politics. While important parts of Keynesian social democracy and free markets can be seen in the policy agenda of New Labour, this should not detract from recognising the ways in which it has carved out a distinct ideological and policy agenda. It is true that some of this has historical forebears. However, an important part of this is novel. This relates particularly to policies fashioned with reference to changes in the global economy. An important part of this overlaps with stakeholding. This book challenges, therefore, a common tendency to dismiss the role stakeholding plays for New Labour. Admittedly, the situation is complex insofar as there is a need to separate out collectivist and individualist stakeholding when making this claim. Nevertheless, both of these strands occupy an important part of the distinct agenda that New Labour has fashioned. New Labour furthermore is likely to draw on collectivist stakeholding as it grapples with the issue of public service reform that is at the heart of its second-term agenda. The replacement of Railtrack with Network Rail in the reform of railways shows signs of this as it overlaps with collectivist stakeholding, insofar as it points to a non-profit-making organisation in which managers are more directly responsible to meeting the needs of consumers. Likewise, greater steps will probably emerge to linking together different parts of its asset-based agenda. None of this is to take up any position for or against such reforms; rather it highlights that it is important to recognise such connections as a precondition for a proper assessment or evaluation of New Labour.

Further directions

The contention of this book, therefore, is that stakeholding does furnish the centre-left with a coherent set of principles of public policy that are compatible with contemporary circumstances and that also differ from Keynesian social democracy and free markets. Moreover it remains important for understanding New Labour. As such, stakeholding is an interesting perspective on public policy and is worthy of further exploration. This may be done in a variety of ways. First, the theoretical discussion of stakeholding can be expanded. A collectivist and individualist distinction has been introduced to help elucidate features of different models. The focus has not been on the evaluation of the relative merits of these different types. One avenue of development looks at whether certain combinations of these types are preferable to others. A second theme further examines the relationship of stakeholding to other components within the third way. This discussion could be expanded by engaging in evaluative analysis alongside the comparative work conducted here, that is, considering the relative strengths and weaknesses of different approaches in third-way space. Another issue looks at ways in which stakeholding could be combined with other components, and the benefits and costs associated with this.

Secondly, the examination of the role stakeholding plays in New Labour can be expanded. Part of this extends the material covered here. One issue relates to how the promise to construct a new pillar in welfare organised around assets unfolds throughout the rest of the second term. Alongside the extension of the existing material, work can also cover the extent to which stakeholding overlaps in areas not covered in this book, for example, health. Although the answers to all the above are difficult to predict with any certainty, one thing is likely to be true. Stakeholding is an important organising framework, and will be an important component in future discussions of British public policy.

Notes

1 The State We're In

1. References to *The State We're In* in this book will refer to the revised second edition (it was originally published by Jonathan Cape in 1995).
2. The extent of consensus can, however, be exaggerated. Robert Leach points out that in this period important ideological differences existed between Labour and the Conservatives about the desirability of collectivist intervention. A broad consensus should not, accordingly, be viewed as implying that complete agreement existed between these parties (Leach 2002).

2 Collectivist Stakeholding

1. Sixteen commissioners staffed *Social Justice*. Chaired by Sir Gordon Borrie QC this included the Warden of Nuffield College, Oxford, A.B. Atkinson FBA; Anita Bhalla of the Asian Resource Centre, Birmingham; John Gennard, Professor of Industrial Relations at Strathclyde University; The Very Reverend John Gladwin, Provost of Sheffield and Bishop-Elect of Guildford; Christopher Haskins, Chairman of Northern Foods plc; deputy chair Patricia Hewitt, Director of Research at Andersen Consulting; Dr Penelope Leach of the British Psychological Society; Ruth Lister, Professor of Social Policy and Administration at Loughborough University; David Marquand, Professor of Politics at Sheffield University; Bert Massie, director of the Royal Association for Disability and Rehabilitation; Emma MacLennan, vice-chair of the Low Pay Unit; Dr Eithne McLaughlin, Reader in Social Policy at Queen's University of Belfast; Steven Webb of the Institute for Fiscal Studies; Margaret Wheeler, director of organisation development at UNISON; and Bernard Williams FBA, White's Professor of Moral Philosophy at the University of Oxford.
2. Chaired by Ralf Dahrendorf, Warden of St Antony's College, Oxford, the other commissioners were Frank Field MP; Carolyn Hayman, Executive Director, Rutherford Ventures; Ian Hutcheson CBE, Chairman and Chief Executive of Acatos & Hutcheson; Will Hutton, Assistant Editor of The Guardian; David Marquand, Professor of Politics, University of Sheffield; Andrew Sentence, Senior Research Fellow, London Business School; and Sir Ian Wrigglesworth, Deputy Chairman John Livingston and Sons Ltd.
3. Chaired by Will Hutton, the other members of the Commission were Conor Gearty, Professor of Human Rights Law at King's College, London; Susie Parsons, Chief Executive of the Commission for Racial Equality; Professor Allyson Pollock, head of the Health Services and Health Policy

Research Unit at University College, London and Director of Research and Development at University College Hospitals Trust; Joyce Struthers, Chair of the Association of Community Health Councils for England and Wales; Professor Stuart Weir, Senior Research Fellow at the Human Rights Centre and Director of the Democratic Audit at the University of Essex; and Stephen Thornton, Chief Executive of the NHS Confederation. Thornton served only until June 1999 because of work commitments, and was replaced from July 1999 by Ken Binmore, Director of the Economic and Social Research Council Centre for Economic Learning and Social Evolution and Leverhulme Research Professor at University College, London.

6 Stakeholding and New Labour

1. Other members included Richard Rogers, Director, Company Law and Investigations, Department of Trade and Industry (Chairman); the Hon. Mrs Justice Arden DBE, High Court Judge, formerly Chairman of the Law Commission; Robert Bertram, formerly partner Shephard and Wedderburn WS; Paul Davis, Professor of Commercial Law, London School of Economics and Political Science; Sir Stuart Hampson, Chairman John Lewis Partnership plc; Colin Perry, Chairman LTE Scientific Ltd, and Chairman, Confederation of British Industry Small and Medium Enterprises Council; Rosemary Radcliffe CBE, Chief Economist, PricewaterhouseCoopers; Jonathan Rickford, Company Law Review Project Director; Bryan Sanderson, Managing Director, BP Amoco Chemicals; Richard Sykes QC formerly of Erskine Chambers; and Martin Scicluna, Chairman, Deloitte and Touche. John Kay was replaced in November 2000 by Sir Bryan Carsberg, Secretary-General, International Accounting Standards Committee.

References

Ackerman, B. and Alstott, A. (1998), *The Stakeholder Society*, New Haven, Yale University Press

Anderson, P. (1964), 'Origins of the present crisis', *New Left Review*, pp. 26–53

Axelrod, R. (1984), *The Evolution of Co-operation*, New York, Basic Books

Baker, K. (ed.) (1993), *The Faber Book of Conservatism*, London, Faber

Banks, J. and Tanner, S. (1999), *Household Saving in the UK*, London, Institute for Fiscal Studies

Bayley, S. (1999), *Labour Camp: the failure of style over substance*, London, Pan Books

Becker, G. (1964), *Human Capital: a theoretical and empirical analysis, with special reference to education*, New York, National Bureau of Economic Research

Bennett, R. and Kelly, J. (2001), 'Pre-Budget Report: training scheme withdrawn early', *Financial Times*, 27 November

Berle, A. and Means, G. (1932), *The Modern Corporation and Private Property*, New York, Macmillan

Blair, M. (1995), *Ownership and Control*, Washington, Brookings Institution

Blair, T. and Schroeder, G. (1999), 'Europe: the third way/die neue mitte', Labour party website <www.labour.org.uk>

Blair, T. (1998), *The Third Way: new politics for a new century*, Fabian pamphlet number 588, London, Fabian Society

Blair, T. (1996), *New Britain: my vision of a young country*, London, Fourth Estate

Butler, D. and Kavanagh, D. (1984), *The British General Election of 1983*, London, Macmillan – now Palgrave Macmillan

Chapman, P. (1998), 'Human capital issues', in Buxton, T., Chapman, P. and Temple, P. (eds), *Britain's Economic Performance*, second edition, London, Routledge, pp. 278–96

Clarke, P. (1978), *Liberals and Social Democrats*, Cambridge, Cambridge University Press

Coates, D. (2000), *Models of Capitalism: growth and stagnation in the modern era*, Cambridge, Polity

Commission on the NHS (2000), *New Life for the NHS*, London, Vintage

Commission on Social Justice (1994), *Social Justice: strategies for national renewal*, London, Vintage

Commission on Wealth Creation and Social Cohesion (1995), *Report on Wealth Creation and Social Cohesion in a Free Society*, London

Company Law Review (2001), *Modern Company Law for a Competitive Economy: final report*, London, Department of Trade and Industry

Company Law Review (2000), *Modern Company Law for a Competitive Economy: developing the framework*, London, Department of Trade and Industry

Company Law Review (1999), *Modern Company Law for a Competitive Economy: the strategic framework*, London, Department of Trade and Industry
Congdon, T. (1997), 'How Britain benefits from short-termism', pp. 19–36, in Hutton, W. (ed.), *Stakeholding and its Critics*, Choice in Welfare no. 36, London, Institute for Economic Affairs
Crequer, N. (2001), 'MPs say "fraud" used to hide Treasury cuts', *Times Education Supplement*, 30 November
Crewe, I. (1993), 'The Thatcher legacy', in King, A. (ed.), *Britain at the Polls 1992*, New Jersey, Chatham House, pp. 1–28
Crosland, C. A. R. (1956), *The Future of Socialism*, London, Jonathan Cape
Crouch, C. and Marquand, D. (1995), 'Reinventing collective action' in Crouch, C. and Marquand, D. (eds), *Reinventing Collective Action: from the global to the local*, Political Quarterly, Oxford, Blackwell, pp. 5–19
Darling, A. (1997), 'A political perspective' in Kelly, G., Kelly, D. and Gamble, A. (eds), *Stakeholder Capitalism*, Basingstoke, Macmillan – now Palgrave Macmillan, pp. 10–19
Department for Education and Employment (1998), *The Learning Age: a renaissance for a new Britain*, London, The Stationery Office
Department of Social Security (1998a), *A New Contract for Welfare: new ambitions for our country*, London, The Stationery Office
Department of Social Security (1998b), *A New Contract for Welfare: the gateway to work*, London, The Stationery Office
Department of Social Security (1998c), *A New Contract for Welfare: support for disabled people*, London, The Stationery Office
Department of Social Security (1998d), *A New Contract for Welfare: partnership in pensions*, London, The Stationery Office
Department of Trade and Industry (2002), *Modernising Company Law*, London, The Stationery Office.
Department of Trade and Industry (2001), *Directors' Remuneration*, London, Department of Trade and Industry
Department of Trade and Industry (1998a), *A Fair Deal for Consumers: modernising the framework for utility regulation*, London, The Stationery Office
Department of Trade and Industry (1998b), *Our Competitive Future: building the knowledge driven economy*, London, The Stationery Office
Desai, M. (1997), 'It's profitability, stupid', in Kelly et al. (eds) (1997), pp. 201–17
Dworkin, R. (2000), *Sovereign Virtue: the theory and practice of equality*, Cambridge, Mass., Harvard University Press
Ellison, N. (1998), 'The changing politics of social policy', in Ellison, N. and Pierson, C. (eds) (1998), *Developments in British Social Policy*, Basingstoke, Macmillan – now Palgrave Macmillan, pp. 31–45
Elster, J. (1996), 'Rationality and Emotions', *Economic Journal*, 106(438), pp. 1386–97
Faulks, K. (2000), *Citizenship*, London, Routledge
Field, F. (2000), *The State of Dependency: welfare under Labour*, London, Social Market Foundation
Field, F. (1998), 'A Hand-up or Put-down for the Poor?', *New Statesman*, 27 November

Field, F. (ed.) (1996a), *Stakeholder Welfare*, London, Institute of Economic Affairs

Field, F. (1996b), 'Staking a claim to power', *The Times*, 9 January

Field, F., Gray, J., Hutton, W., Kay, J. and Marquand, D. (1996), 'Tony and the Tories: this is what we mean', *Observer*, 7 July

Finegold, D. and Soskice, D. (1988), 'The failure of training in Britain: analysis and prescription', *Oxford Review of Economic Policy*, 4(3), pp. 23–43

Freeman, R. E. (1984), *Strategic Management: a stakeholder approach*, Boston, Pitman

Fukuyama, F. (1992), *The End of History and the Last Man*, London, Hamish Hamilton

Gamble, A. (2000), *Politics and Fate*, Cambridge, Polity

Gamble, A. (1996a), *Hayek: the iron cage of liberty*, Cambridge, Polity

Gamble, A. (1992), 'The Labour party and economic management' in Smith, M. J. and Spear, J. (1992), *The Changing Labour Party*, London, Routledge, pp. 61–88

Gamble, A. and Kelly, G. (1998), 'Let's Talk About Real Fan Power', *New Statesman*, 27 March, p. 28

Gamble, A. and Kelly, G. (1996a), 'The politics of ownership', *New Left Review*, 220 (Nov/Dec), pp. 62–97

Gamble, A. and Kelly, G. (1996b), 'Stakeholder capitalism and one nation socialism', *Renewal*, 4(1), pp. 23–32

Gamble, A. and Wright, T. (1999), 'Introduction: the new social democracy', in Gamble, A. and Wright, T. (eds), *The New Social Democracy*, Oxford, Blackwell, pp. 1–9

Giddens, A. (1999), *Runaway World: how globalisation is shaping our lives*, London, Profile

Giddens, A. (1998), *The Third Way: the renewal of social democracy*, Cambridge, Polity

Glyn, A. and Miliband, D. (1994), *Paying for Inequality*, London, Institute for Public Policy Research

Goldblatt, D. (ed.) (1999), *The Stakeholding Society: writings on politics and economics*, Cambridge, Polity

Gray, J. (1997) 'After Social Democracy' in Gray, J. (1997) (ed.), *Endgames: questions in late modern political thought*, Cambridge, Polity, pp. 11–50

Harden, I. and Marquand, D. (1997), 'How to make quangos democratic', in Flinders, M., Harden, I. and Marquand, D. (eds) (1997), *How to Make Quangos Democratic*, Charter 88, London (in association with Political Economy Research Centre, University of Sheffield), pp. 8–30

Hart, O. (1995), 'Corporate Governance: some theory and implications', *Economic Journal*, 105, pp. 678–89

Hay, C. (1999), *The Political Economy of New Labour: labouring under false pretences?* Manchester, Manchester University Press

Hay, C. (1996), 'A state of disarray? Huttonomics, New Labour, and the contemporary British impasse', *Renewal*, 4(3), pp. 40–51

Hay, C. and Watson, M. (1998), 'In the dedicated pursuit of dedicated capital: restoring an indigenous investment ethic to British capitalism', *New Political Economy*, 3(3), pp. 407–26

Hayek, F. (1976), *Law, Legislation and Liberty: a new statement of the liberal principles of justice and political economy*: vol. 2: *The Mirage of Social Justice*, London, Routledge

Hayek, F. (1967), *Studies in Philosophy, Politics and Economics*, London, Routledge & Kegan Paul

Hayes, M. (1994), *The New Right in Britain: an introduction to theory and practice*, London, Pluto Press

Heffernan, R. (2001), *New Labour and Thatcherism: political change in Britain*, Basingstoke, Palgrave – now Palgrave Macmillan

Hirst, P. (1994), *Associative Democracy: new forms of economic and social governance*, Cambridge, Polity

Hirst, P. and Thompson, G. (1996), *Globalisation in Question: the international economy and the possibility of governance*, Cambridge, Polity

HM Treasury (2002), *The Strength to Make Long-Term Decisions: investing in an enterprising, fairer Britain*, London, The Stationery Office

HM Treasury (2001a), *Building a Stronger, Fairer Britain in an Uncertain World*, London, The Stationery Office

HM Treasury (2001b), *Investing for the Long-Term: building opportunity and prosperity for all*, London, The Stationery Office

HM Treasury (2000a), *Prudent for a Purpose: building opportunity and security for all: 2000 spending review: new public spending plans 2001–2004*, Command paper 4807, London, The Stationery Office

HM Treasury (2000b), *Prudent for a Purpose: working for a stronger and fairer Britain*, House of Commons paper 346, London, The Stationery Office

HM Treasury (2000c), *Building Long-Term Prosperity for All*, Command paper 4917, London, The Stationery Office

HM Treasury (1999), *Pre-Budget Summary Leaflet: stability and steady growth for Britain*, London, HM Treasury

Hobhouse, L.T. (1911), *Liberalism*, London, Williams & Norgate

Hodgson, G. (1999), *Economic and Utopia: why the learning economy is not the end of history*, London, Routledge

Holland, S. (1975), *The Socialist Challenge*, London, Quartet

Holtham, G. (1997) *Labour and the Private Sector: is stakeholding a big idea?* Policy Paper no. 1, Sheffield, Political Economy Research Centre, University of Sheffield

Holtham, G. and Kay, J. (1994), 'The assessment: institutions of policy', *Oxford Review of Economic Policy* 10(3), pp. 1–16

Honore, A.M. (1961), 'Ownership' in Guest, A. G. (ed.), *Oxford Essays in Jurisprudence*, Oxford, Oxford University Press, pp. 107–47

Hook, S. (2002), 'Ministers still back son of ILA', *Times Education Supplement*, 5 July 2002

Huntington, N. and Bale, T. (2002), 'New Labour: New Christian Democracy?' *Political Quarterly*, 73(1), pp. 44–50

Hutton, W. (2000a), 'Will Hutton' in English, R. and Kenny, M. (eds), *Rethinking British Decline*, Basingstoke, Macmillan – now Palgrave Macmillan, pp. 50–60

Hutton, W. (2000b), 'Towards a juster capitalism', *New Statesman* Special Supplement, 6 November, pp. v–vi
Hutton, W. (1999), 'Afterword', in Goldblatt, D. (ed.) (1999), *The Stakeholding Society: writings on politics and economics*, Cambridge, Polity, pp. 267–74
Hutton, W. (1997a), 'The stakeholder society', *Stakeholding and its Critics*, London, Institute of Economic Affairs, Choice in Welfare series no. 36, pp. 1–16
Hutton, W. (1997b), 'An overview of stakeholding', in Kelly et al. (eds) (1997), pp. 3–9
Hutton, W. (1996), *The State We're In*, London, Vintage
Hutton, W. and Kay, J. (1996), 'Only working together will save the economy', *Observer* 13 October
Kavanagh, D. (1997), *The Re-ordering of British Politics: politics after Thatcherism*, Oxford, Oxford University Press, chapter 10
Kay, J. (2001), 'A new public sector', *Prospect*, June
Kay, J. (1997a), 'The stakeholder corporation', in Kelly et al. (eds) (1997), pp. 125–41
Kay, J. (1997b), 'The ethics of stakeholding', *New Times*, 26 April, pp. 6–7
Kay, J. (1997c), 'A stakeholding society – what does it mean for business?' *Scottish Journal of Political Economy*, 44(4), pp. 425–36
Kay, J. (1996a), 'Staking a moral claim', *New Statesman*, 11 October, pp. 18–20
Kay, J. (1996b), 'The good market', *Prospect*, May, pp. 39–43
Kay, J. (1996c), 'The future of UK utility regulation', in Beesley. M. E. (ed.), *Regulating Utilities: a time for change?* London, Institute of Economic Affairs, pp. 145–75
Kay, J. (1996d), The Business of Economics, Oxford, Oxford University Press
Kay, J. (1994a), 'Corporate strategy and accountability', in Dimsdale, N. and Prevezer, M. (eds) (1994), *Capital Markets and Corporate Governance*, Oxford, Clarendon, pp. 50–65
Kay, J. (1994b), *The Foundations of Corporate Success*, Oxford, Oxford University Press
Kay, J. (1994c), 'The competitive advantage of nations', Economic and Social Research Council Annual Lecture, reprinted in Kay, J. (1996d), pp. 69–80
Kay, J. (1993), *Foundations of Corporate Success*, Oxford, Oxford University Press
Keasey, K., Thompson, S. and Wright, M. (1997), 'Introduction', in Keasey, K., Thompson, S. and Wright, M. (eds) (1997), *Corporate Governance: economic, management and financial issues*, Oxford, Oxford University Press, pp. 1–17
Keep, E. and Mayhew, K. (1998), 'Vocational education and training and economic performance' in Buxton, T., Chapman, P. and Temple, P. (eds), *Britain's Economic Performance*, London: Routledge, pp. 367–98
Kelly, G. (2000), 'All shall have wealth', *New Statesman*, 14 February, pp. 21–2
Kelly, G. (1997), 'Review of Plender', *Renewal*, 5(3/4), Autumn
Kelly, G., Kelly, D. and Gamble, A. (1997), 'Conclusion: stakeholder capitalism' in Kelly, G., Kelly, D. and Gamble, A. (eds), *'Stakeholder Capitalism'*, Basingstoke, Macmillan – now Palgrave Macmillan, pp. 238–56

Kelly, G. and Lissauer, R. (2000), *Ownership for All*, London, Institute for Public Policy Research

Kelly, G. and Parkinson, J. (2001), 'The conceptual foundations of the company: a pluralist approach', in Parkinson, J., Gamble, A. and Kelly, G. (eds), *The Political Economy of the Company*, London, Hart Publishing, pp. 113–39

Kenny, M. and Smith, M. J. (2001), 'Interpreting new Labour: constraints, dilemmas and political agency', in Ludlam, S. and Smith, M. J. (eds), *New Labour in Government*, Basingstoke, Macmillan – now Palgrave Macmillan, pp. 234–55

Keynes, J. M. (1936), *The General Theory of Employment, Interest and Money*, London, Macmillan

King, D. and Wickham-Jones, M. (1999), 'Bridging the Atlantic: the Democratic (Party) origins of welfare to work', in Powell, M. (ed) (1999), *New Labour, New Welfare State?* London, Policy Press, pp. 257–80

Labour Party (2001), *Ambitions for Britain*, London, Labour Party

Labour Party (1997), *New Labour: because Britain deserves better*, London, Labour Party

Layard, R. (1997), *What Labour Can Do*, London, Fontana

Leach, R. (2002), *Political Ideology in Britain*, Basingstoke, Macmillan – now Palgrave Macmillan

Leadbeater, C. (2000), *Living on Thin Air: the new economy*, London, Penguin

Leadbeater, C. and Mulgan, G. (1996a), 'Comment and analysis: Labour's forgotten idea – personal view', *Financial Times*, 2 October

Leadbeater, C. and Mulgan, G. (1996b), *Mistakeholding – whatever happened to Labour's big idea*, London, Demos

Le Grand, J. (1997), 'Knights, knaves or pawns? Human behaviour and social policy', *Journal of Social Policy*, vol. 26, pp. 149–69

Le Grand, J. and Nissan, D. (2000), *A Capital Idea: start-up grants for young people*, Policy Report no. 49, London, The Fabian Society

Le Grand, J. and Nissan, D. (1999), 'A birthday gift for every teenager', *New Statesman*, 4 October, pp. 25–7

Levitas, R. (1998), *The Inclusive Society? Social Exclusion and New Labour*, Basingstoke, Macmillan – now Palgrave Macmillan

Lordon, F. (1998), 'The logic and limits of désinflation compétitive', *Oxford Review of Economic Policy*, 14(1), pp. 96–113

Ludlam, S. (2000), 'New Labour: what's published is what counts', *British Journal of Politics and International Relations*, 2(2), pp. 264–76

Macfarlane, L. (1996), 'Socialism and common Ownership: an historical perspective', in King, P. (ed) (1996), *Socialism and the Common Good: new Fabian essays*, London, Cass, pp. 17–61

Maltby, J. and Wilkinson, R. (1998), 'Stakeholding and corporate governance', *Politics*, 18(3), pp. 197–204

Mandelson, P. and Liddle, R. (1996), *The Blair Revolution: Can New Labour Deliver?* London, Faber & Faber

Margetts, H. and Smyth, G. (eds) (1994), *Turning Japanese? Britain with Permanent Party of Government*, London, Lawrence & Wishart

Marquand, D. (2001), 'Can Blair kill off Britain's Tory state at last?', *New Statesman*, pp. 19–20

Marquand, D. (2000), 'The fall of civic culture', *New Statesman*, 13 November, pp. 27–9

Marquand, D. (1999a), *The Progressive Dilemma*, second edition, London, Phoenix

Marquand, D. (1999b), 'Premature obsequies: social democracy comes in from the cold', in Gamble, A. and Wright, T. (eds) (1999) *The New Social Democracy*, Blackwell, Oxford, pp. 10–20

Marquand, D. (1998a), *Must Labour Win?*, transcript of 9th Economic and Social Research Council Annual Lecture, Swindon

Marquand, D. (1998b), 'Rethinking pluralism', *New Times*, 28 March, p. 8

Marquand, D. (1997), *The New Reckoning*, Cambridge, Polity

Marquand, D. (1996) The Stakeholder Society, http://www.netnexus.org/library/papers/marquand.htm 6/6/99

Marquand, D. (1988), *The Unprincipled Society: new demands and old politics*, London, Jonathan Cape

Marshall, T. H. (1950), *Citizenship and Social Class*, Cambridge, Cambridge University Press

Mayo, E. and Moore, H. (2001), *The Mutual State: how local communities can run public services*, London, New Economics Foundation

Mead, L. (1986), *Beyond Entitlement: the social obligations of citizenship*, New York, Free Press

Monks, J. (1996), 'The TUC's stake in Mr Blair', *The Times*, 17 January

Myners, P. (2001) *Institutional Investment in the UK: a review*, London, HM Treasury

Niskanen, W. A. (1971), *Bureaucracy and Representative Government*, Chicago, Aldine-Atherton

Paine, T. (1987), 'Agrarian justice', in Foot, M. and Kramnick, I. (eds) (1987), *The Thomas Paine Reader*, London, Penguin

Parkinson, J. (1997a), 'Company law and stakeholder governance', in Kelly et al. (eds) (1997), pp. 142–54

Parkinson, J. (1997b), *Reforming Directors' Duties*, Policy Paper no. 12, Political Economy Research Centre, University of Sheffield, Sheffield

Peacock, A. and Wiseman, J. (1961), *The Growth of Public Expenditure in the United Kingdom*, Princeton, Princeton University Press

Perraton, J., Goldblatt, D., Held, D. and McGrew, A. (1997), 'The globalisation of economic activity', *New Political Economy*, 2(2), pp. 257–77

Plant, R. (2001), 'Blair and ideology', in Seldon, A. (ed.) (2001), pp. 555–68

Plant. R. (1996), 'Social Democracy', in Marquand, D. and Seldon, A. (eds) (1996), pp. 139–64

Plender, J. (1997), *A Stake in the Future: the stakeholding solution*, London, Nicholas Brearly

Porter, M. E. (1990), *The Competitive Advantage of Nations*, Basingstoke, Macmillan – now Palgrave Macmillan

Putnam, R. (2000), *Bowling Alone: the collapse and revival of American community*, New York, Simon & Schuster

Putnam, R., Leonardi, R. and Nanetti, R. Y. (1993), *Making Democracy Work: civic traditions in modern Italy*, Princeton, Princeton University Press

Ramsden, J. (1980), *The Making of Conservative Party Policy: the Conservative research department since 1929*, London, Longman

Redwood, J. (1988), *Popular Capitalism*, London, Routledge

Reich, R. (1992), *The Work of Nations: preparing ourselves for 21st century capitalism*, New York, Vintage Books

Rhenman, E. (1967), *Industrial Democracy and Industrial Management: a critical essay on the possible meanings and implications of industrial democracy*, London, Tavistock

Sen, A. (1990), 'Rational Fools: a critique of the behavioral foundations of economic theory' in Mansbridge, J. (ed.) *Beyond Self-Interest*, Chicago, University of Chicago Press, pp. 25–43

Shaw, E. (1994), *The Labour Party Since 1979: crisis and transformation*, London, Routledge

Sherraden, M. (1991), *Assets and the Poor, A New American Welfare Policy*, New York, Sharpe

Sherraden, M. (1990), 'Stakeholding – notes on a theory of welfare based on assets', *Social Service Review*, 64(4), pp. 580–601

Sherraden, M., Page-Adams, D. and Johnson, L. (1999), *Downpayments on the American Dream Policy Demonstration: a national demonstration of individual development accounts*, St Louis, Washington University in St. Louis, Center for Social Development

Skidelsky, R. (2000), 'A stake in the heart', *Times Literary Supplement*, 21 January, p. 8

Skidelsky, R. (1996), 'Thatcher's unfinished business', *Prospect*, pp. 38–45

Smith, A. (1993), *An Enquiry into the Nature and Causes of the Wealth of Nations*, Oxford, Oxford University Press

Smith, A. (1976), *The Theory of Moral Sentiments*, Oxford, Oxford University Press

Smith, M. J. (1992), 'A return to revisionism? The Labour party's policy review', in Smith, M. J. and Spear, J. (eds) (1992), *The Changing Labour Party*, London, Routledge, pp. 13–28

Solomon, R. C. (1992), *Ethics and Excellence: co-operation and integrity in business*, Oxford, Oxford University Press

Soskice, D. (1999), 'Divergent production regimes: coordinated and uncoordinated market economies in the 1980s and 1990s', in Kitschelt, H., Lange, P., Marks, G. and Stephens, J. D. (eds) (1999), *Continuity and Change in Contemporary Capitalism*, Cambridge, Cambridge University Press, pp. 101–34

Soskice, D. (1997), 'Stakeholding yes, German model no' in Kelly et al. (eds) (1997), pp. 219–25

Sternberg, E. (1998), *Corporate Governance: accountability in the marketplace*, Hobart paper 137, London, Institute of Economic Affairs

Tullock, G. (1976), *The Vote Motive*, London, Institute of Economic Affairs

Varian, H. (1990), *Intermediate Microeconomics: a modern approach*, second edition, New York, W. W. Norton

Vickers, J. and Yarrow, G. (1988), *Privatization: an economic analysis*, Cambridge, Massachusetts, MIT Press

Webster, P. (1996), 'TUC chief hails boost for unions', *The Times*, 17 January

Webster, P. (1996), 'TUC chief hails boost for unions', *The Times*, 17 January
Webster, P. and Sherman, J. (1996), 'Give all workers shares in their firms say Labour', *The Times*, 18 January
White, S. (2000), 'Social rights and the social contract – political theory and the new welfare politics', *British Journal of Political Science*, 30, pp. 507–32
White, S. (1999), 'Rights and responsibilities: a social democratic perspective', in Gamble, A. and Wright, T. (1999) (eds), pp. 166–79
White, S. (1998) 'Interpreting the third way: not one route but many', *Renewal*, 6(2), pp. 17–30
White, S. (1997), 'What do egalitarians want?' in Franklin, J. (ed.) (1997) *Equality*, London, Institute for Public Policy Research, pp. 59–82
Williamson, J. (1997), 'Your stake at work: the TUC's agenda', in Kelly et al. (eds) (1997), pp. 155–68
Williamson, O. (1985), *The Economic Institutions of Capitalism*, New York, Free Press
Willetts, D. (1997), 'Civic conservatism', pp. 69–141 and 'Conclusion', pp. 167–80 in Willetts, D. and Gray, J. (eds) (1997), *Is Conservatism Dead?* London, Social Market Foundation
Willetts, D. (1996), 'Why Blair is no heir to Thatcher', *The Times*, 11 January
Willetts, D. (1992), *Modern Conservatism*, London, Penguin

Index